20YEARS Communications

20 Leaders, 20 Questions, 100's of Lessons

Written and Directed by Kevin Popović

Edited by Marshal D. Carper

Contributing Authors

Paige Beal
Brian Bronaugh
Roy Cheran
Rob Deaner
Don Decker
Guido D'Elia
Bill Flanagan
Michael Hills
Rick Landesberg
Mike Lee
Michael Lotenero
Saul Markowitz
Dennis Moran
Raelin Sawka Musuraca
Glenn Przyborski
Chauncey Smith
Julie Smith
David Sladack
Jack Wolf

An Ideahaus Business Book

20YEARS Communications

20 Leaders, 20 Questions, 100's of Lessons

For information regarding special discounts for bulk and academic
purchases please contact Transmedia Books Special Sales
at 1-858-756-5767 or sales@TransmediaBooks.com.

Transmedia Books
360 Nueces St., Suite 2405
Austin, TX 78701

Manufactured in the United States of America

Library of Congress Control Number: 2013942538

ISBN-10: 0989555046
ISBN-13: 978-0-9895550-4-3

Behind the scenes of the *20YEARS Communications* video series.
Photo courtesy of Jack Wolf.

Praise For 20YEARS Communications

"20YEARS sheds considerable light on all types of communications... Don't miss this book and the smart, talented, accomplished and very opinionated professionals whose insights reside within."

"In my 34years in the business, I don't know too many people who could have pulled this off. To muster the forces of this many thought leaders, from so many different areas of our business, and extract from them these kinds of insights and admonitions and perspectives and sheer brilliance is truly a feat of herculean proportions. As much as this business has changed, it's not always changed for the better. As much as this business has changed, it's also stayed fundamentally the same (though you'll get few social media apologists to admit to this). This book sheds considerable light on all of it, from the important to the inane, from the ridiculous to the sublime. And at the heart of it all–just where you'd expect to find him–is Kevin Popović: instigator, visionary anarchist and ringmaster extraordinaire. Don't miss this book and the smart, talented, accomplished and opinionated professionals whose insights reside within. We may never see their like again, given where this business is going."

-George Evans, Principal & Creative Director
Brandwidth

"20YEARS Communications provides a valuable perspective of the past two decades, and more importantly, what the future holds for those working in marketing communications."

"Those who work in various areas of marketing communications often tend to approach problems from the perspective of their particular specialty rather than focusing on integration. This approach may have worked well in the past when the various communication tools available to marketers were limited. However, today the marketer's tool box is growing exponentially rather than incrementally given all of the advances in digital technology. 20YEARS Communications provides a valuable perspective regarding the changes that have occurred over the past two decades, and more importantly, what the future holds for those working in marketing communications."

-George Belch, Prof. / Chair, Dept. of Marketing
San Diego State University

"Those who read 20YEARS will have a significant advantage over most who are just going through marketing by trial and error."

"For all of us in marketing, let alone digital, it's a forgone conclusion that the breadth of areas we need to stay abreast of is overwhelming–Social Media, PR, Branding, Digital and so on–so, for me it's really great to see a book like *20YEARS Communications* that covers such a wide array of topics and in a digestible way that ties all areas into one cohesive way to think. One can't help but think, 'those that read this will have a significant advantage over most who are just going through marketing by trial and error. And that business results will most definitely ensue.'"

-Aaron Kahlow, CEO & Founder
Online Marketing Institute

"The professionals answering the questions on the various topics are FABULOUS. Thank you – Thank you – Thank you for your dedication to your craft."

"I have been in the advertising and marketing world for 30 years as a freelance commercial talent—20 years of which was spent as under contract as the "Shop 'N Save Lady—and as an independent producer and writer. I came to a *20YEARS* event to hear Kevin Popović from Ideahaus and Brian Bronaugh from Mullen. The videos are filled with so much content that I find myself watching again and again and recommending *20YEARS* to other business owners. The panelists answering the questions on the various topics are fabulous. To the panelists and the individuals behind *The 20YEARS Project*: Thank you – Thank you – Thank you for your dedication to your craft."

-Kathy Svilar, On-Camera Talent, Writer / Producer

"Over the last 20 years we've seen dramatic advancements in the ways we communicate, from a traditional platform to digital environments. Integrating communications followed by engagement is key to taking advantage of how far we've come and how far we are yet to go."

"Communication remains the fundamental touchstone for business and education, and it always will. Over the last 20 years in particular, we have seen dramatic advancements in the ways in which we communicate, from a predominantly traditional platform, now to expanding digital environments that give customers a voice without the letters-to-the editors and telephone trees of yesteryear. But for business, communication is only half of the task; the other half is listening. Integrating communications followed by engagement is key to taking advantage of how far we've come and how far we are yet to go."

-Jeffrey Hayzlett, Global Business Celebrity, Bloomberg TV Contributing Editor, Bestselling Author, Speaker & Sometime Cowboy

Kevin Popović and Tom Dressler, Kevin Popovic Image Design
The Brew House, Pittsburgh, PA circa 1990
Credit: Pittsburgh Business Times, March 1991

Paul Shapiro, Jeff Jarzynka and Kevin Popović, Ideahaus
East Carson Street Studio, Pittsburgh, PA circa 1995
Credit: Pittsburgh Tribune-Review, April 1995

Acknowledgments

There are a number of people I'd like to acknowledge who have contributed to my personal development, my education and the advancement of my career, which has all lead to this project.

Thanks to my mother, **Judy Reed**, for sharing your creativity and work ethic.

Thanks to my father, **Dr. Charles Popovich**, for teaching me what you know and providing a never-ending source of support.

Thanks to **Frank Klapak** and **Grace Fratangelo** for the introduction to communications and the latitude to follow my curiosity.

Thank you, **Bob Friday**, for providing a mentor when I needed one.

Thank you, **Thomas P. Dressler III,** for starting an agency with me (pictured left). Thanks to **Jeff Jarzynka** and **Paul Shapiro** (also pictured left) for helping me grow it even more.

Thanks to **Dr. Ron Hansen, Dr. John Shepherd** and **Dr. Larry Tomei** for the opportunity to teach and to continue my education.

Thanks to every client that provided me an opportunity to do what I love, and to every colleague that helped me learn just a little more.

Thanks to my contributing authors for sharing your wisdom and to our editor, **Marshal D. Carper**, for making some sense of this all.

Thank you, **Amy King,** for the production value you added to the 20YEARS Project, and to **Rob Deaner** for the music that so brilliantly set our stage.

Thank you, everyone. - kp

Author / Director Kevin Popović on the set of *20YEARS Communications*.
Photo courtesy of Jack Wolf.

About the 20YEARS Project

Remember 1990?

I do, like it was yesterday, because we were all incredibly excited about what was happening in communications. New technologies were emerging that revolutionized the way people connect and share information.

On the 20th anniversary of Ideahaus, I reflected on how much has changed since I got into the communications business, and as I discussed my revelations with colleagues with the same tenure I realized everyone had experiences of their own from their perspective to share as well.

I remember thinking, somebody should record this. And we did. The 20YEARS Project was based on issues selected by senior creative and communications professionals. The project is structured around a series of key questions that explores issues and experiences that all communications professionals encounter in their careers. It also shares with aspiring artists, writers, designers, producers, and strategists some critical insights that reflect the changing styles, strategy, and media of the last 20 years.

Our Partners in Production

The 20YEARS Project was directed by Ideahaus Founder & CEO Kevin Popović, and produced by Amy King and the team at Mind Over Media. Original music for the project was produced by Rob Deaner and Market Street Sound. Event marketing was shared between partner organizations, including Pittsburgh Ad Fed (AAF), Pittsburgh Chapter of American Institute of Graphic Artists (AIGA), Media Association of Pittsburgh (MAP), Pittsburgh 12 20YEARS Communications Chapter of Public Relations Society of America (PRSA) and Pittsburgh Technical Institute (PTI).

Why look back at 20 years of communications?

As we talked about Ideahaus' anniversary, our original studios, and who got started in the business at the same time, we realized that we all had to make a series of uninformed decisions when we got into the communications business. Some of the dilemmas we faced:

- Join an agency or start my own?
- Stick to my art or get a steady job?
- Go client-side or stay in production?
- Stay at home or get out of town?

When I asked my colleagues how it has all worked out for them, I began to uncover startling stories and endless retrospective insights, and I realized that we had to record this knowledge. Notable communications professionals from every discipline have been invited to participate in *20YEARS* and to speak from their vantage points. Each panelist has been in the business for at least 20 years and are accomplished in their space.

Some key details to stress: First, this is about communications–all types of communications. Advertising, marketing, design, public relations, multimedia, events – all of them. When I started my agency, it was about communications. Twenty years later, it's about communications. Traditionally, a lot of these things have been treated as though they are worlds apart. I believe this project will show how much more we all have in common, how we all fit together, how we are all really trying to do the same thing – and that's help somebody communicate to somebody else.

The content from the project was originally released during a preview event in Pittsburgh, PA during the celebration of Ideahaus' 20th anniversary.

The book was developed as a guide through the project, a compliment to the workshops and presentations, and a resource for academic courses.

Join Our Conversation

Please accept our invitation to join this conversation.

Read the book, consider the context of the comments, and watch the video to help form your own opinion.

Each question in the book has a QR code which, when scanned with a QR code reader, links to a video presentation of the panelists' commentary. This QR code links to the 20YEARS Project website at http://ideahaus.com/20years.

Share your comments to help build a better understanding to the ongoing conversations on our website or by following #20yearsbook on social media.

Inside 20YEARS Communications

Popović interviews contributors using an Interrotron to capture eye contact on camera. Photo courtesy of Jack Wolf.

Introduction

20 years, 20 experts, 20 questions—this was the basis for the 20YEARS Project.

Between 1990 and 2010, communications experienced a radical amount of change. In that period, technological innovation inspired a shift in culture that revolutionized the way that we communicate. As technology, software and services entered the market with greater frequency, consumers adopted new habits and abandoned old ones.

Opportunities were numerous but so too were challenges and uncertainties. Communication was at the same time converging on a mobile platform and splintering into countless new channels and communities, each preferred to different degrees by different audiences. A certain "communitivity" was born from a collision of these new communications channels, and a newfound sense of interactivity stimulated our culture. Technology expanded to reveal new opportunities, both synchronous and asynchronous, with the impact arguably equal to the likes of Gutenberg's press, Morse code or television.

And this trend continues today.

Our panelists represent the full scope of communications—from photographers to professors to partners—and not only did they witness the evolution of communications, they were in the field and in the boardroom, brainstorming ways to leverage new developments and overcome new obstacles.

Their knowledge and their experience are invaluable, and they provide a diverse front line perspective that is missing in most books written about communications. By assembling them into one conversation, you can see how professionals with various specialties think about communications and learn how they perceive the various facets of the industry, making this book a great companion to a college class or a tool for facilitating team-building discussion within an agency or department.

How to Use This Book

As you read through this book, answer our questions yourself and see how your answers compare to the answers of our panelists.

Use the discussion questions at the end of each chapter to probe themes and topics more deeply. Talk to your colleagues and peers about what you have read and learn from their perspective, just as we have, while at the same time challenging each other to see things from a different perspective.

Follow #20yearsbook throughout social media for ongoing insights, comments and conversations. Post your comments, questions and experiences to contribute towards the creation of a common understanding.

Learn from #20YEARSBOOK

By looking back at the last 20 years, and by engaging with our panelists, you can prepare yourself, your company, and your communications for the next 20 years. Contribute your thoughts and join our ongoing conversations with other readers in our archive at http://ideahaus.com/20YEARS.

Kevin Popović

About the Authors

"I once got a fortune cookie that read, 'None of us know as much as all of us.' So if we're going to get the big picture, then we better invite everyone." - Kevin Popović

There's a lot of people in the communications community that have experiences just like yours. And there's even more that have nothing in common at all. The intent of *20YEARS* is to make sure that every aspect, every facet, and every opinion is represented.

And to learn about the last 20 years, to really learn about and explore the multiple facets of what has happened in all of communications, we invited 20 voices from every channel of communications.

Meet our panelists.

Kevin Popović is the Founder & CEO of Ideahaus, a boutique creative communications agency with studios in Pittsburgh and San Diego. Since 1990, Kevin has been helping clients figure out "what to say and how to say it" to their target markets.

Kevin has been an Adjunct Professor at Duquesne University teaching multimedia and communications to undergraduate, graduate, and continuing education students. He also developed and delivered corporate training for Fortune 500 companies.

Popović is the creator of "Satellite Marketing," a trademarked strategy for using social media for business, and has authored academic articles and original research. In 2010, Kevin was ranked #43 in Fast Company's *The Influence Project* measuring "the most influential people online."

Connect With the Author

Scan this QR code to connect with Kevin Popović on LinkedIn, follow @KevinPopovic or visit http://ideahaus.com.

Paige Beal specializes in entertainment marketing, media marketing, marketing research, emerging technology, and the impact of these efforts on consumer behavior. Her career spans radio, television, and academia.

As an Associate Professor at the Point Park University School of Business for 11 years, Paige taught graduate and undergraduate courses in advertising and marketing and also taught specialty courses in Internet marketing and media management.

Her work as a professor earned her the American Marketing Association Distinguished Educator Award, and her professional work earned her the Media Association of Pittsburgh Art Stein Award as well as awards for Best Media Professional and Best Internet Professional.

Connect with this Contributor

Scan this QR code to connect with Paige Beal on LinkedIn or follow @paigebeal on Twitter.

Brian Bronaugh is the president and executive creative director at Mullen Pittsburgh, a globally recognized marketing firm with offices in Boston, Los Angeles, San Francisco, Pittsburgh, North Carolina, and New York.

At Mullen, Brian works to simplify all of the complexities brands face into a riveting and approachable message that "invites conversation, earns trial, grows sales, and builds loyalty." Working with companies such as Highmark Blue Cross Blue Shield, American Diabetes Association, and Magellan GPS, Brian has established himself as one of Pittsburgh's most influential marketers.

Since 1990, Brian has played a vital role in Mullen's growth from a successful creative boutique to the global operation it is today, a testament to his dedication and his ability to adapt to the ever-changing communications landscape.

Connect with this Contributor

Scan this QR code to connect with Brian Bronaugh on LinkedIn or visit http://www.mullen.com.

Roy Cheran serves as the Vice President of Marketing & Sales at TowerCare Technologies, a Pennsylvania-based company which effectively brings together fundraising, constituent management, donation tracking, and work flow management in one extremely user-friendly package.

Previously, Roy worked for 13 years as the director of business development at Mind Over Media, specializing in helping industry-leading Fortune 500 companies such as Xerox, Emerson, and Dick's Sporting Goods develop message strategies which utilize integrated marketing and media tools.

For his outstanding work in the field of marketing and communications, Roy is a Presidential C-Flag Citation Recipient for private sector initiatives, CASE Award winner, and two-time recipient of the Gold Award through the Association of Incentive Marketing.

Connect with this Contributor

Scan this QR code to connect with Roy Cheran on LinkedIn or visit http://towercare.com.

Rob Deaner is a Partner at Market Street Sound in Pittsburgh where he serves as a music producer, composer, and mixer. Market Street Sound has worked with several high-level artists and serves the creative and advertising industries.

Rob is also the President of the Pittsburgh Advertising Federation and has worked at large post-production facilities such as Atlantic Teleproductions and TPC, both of which are located in Pittsburgh.

While living in New York City, he worked with artists such as Billy Idol, John Waite, and Rachel Z, as well as many top producers and writers.

Connect with this Contributor

Scan this QR code to connect with Rob Deaner on LinkedIn or visit http://www.marketstreetsound.com.

Don Decker is a television advertising professional from Pittsburgh with almost 25 years of experience in the market.

Don currently serves as an Account Executive at WPXI in Pittsburgh where he develops integrated campaigns and produces advertising content for local businesses.

Previously, he worked in similar positions with Comcast Spotlight, KDKA-AM, and Clear Channel Communications. His extensive career in television has made him a sought-after expert on television advertising.

Connect with this Contributor

Scan this QR code to connect with Don Decker on LinkedIn or visit http://www.wpxi.com.

Guido D'Elia is the Co-Founder and Senior Strategist at Mind Over Media, a research, strategy, and production firm, where he has served for over 30 years. He also serves as a Consultant for G, a sports marketing and communications consultancy firm in State College, Pennsylvania.

Guido previously served as the Director of Communications and Branding for Football and Penn State University for eight years and worked in a variety of positions with TPC Communications early in his career.

While at Penn State, he inspired many ideas and practices that are now popular game-day traditions at Beaver Stadium.

Connect with this Contributor

Scan this QR code to connect with Guido D'Elia on LinkedIn or visit http://www.momknows.com.

Bill Flanagan has acted as the Executive Vice President of Corporate Relations for the Allegheny Conference on Community Development since 2001 and also hosts the television show "Our Region's Business" on WPXI in Pittsburgh.

As President of the G-20 Partnership which organized private sector host organizations, Bill played a crucial role in the Pittsburgh G-20 Summit. He has also served as the Money Editor for KDKA-TV in Pittsburgh for almost 20 years and, more recently, as the Director of Leadership Pittsburgh, Inc.

He holds a bachelor's degree from Northwestern University and a master's degree in journalism from the University of Missouri-Columbia.

Connect with this Contributor

Scan this QR code to connect with Bill Flanagan on LinkedIn or visit http://www.alleghenyconference.org.

Michael Hills is the Vice President and General Manager at Comcast Spotlight where he is responsible for overseeing large advertising markets in Pennsylvania, West Virginia, and Ohio. He has worked at Comcast since 2000 and now manages over 100 employees.

Before working with Comcast, Michael was with Sinclair Communications in Pittsburgh and Sacramento where he served in broadcast television sales management for 12 years.

He was recognized as the Best Sales Manager in 2002, 2003, and 2004 by the Media Association of Pittsburgh and was also recognized as the Best Overall Professional in television in 2005. He also received the first Cable Advertising Sales Management Award from the Cable Television Bureau in 2002.

Connect with this Contributor

Scan this QR code to connect with Michael Hills on LinkedIn or visit http://www.comcastspotlight.com/markets/pittsburgh.

Mike Lee is a noted television host, film producer, and founder of StudiousOne Digital Film Arts, a Pittsburgh-based visual production company. In addition to his work at StudiousOne, Mike is a producer and reporter for WQED Multimedia and served as the Vice President of Business Development and Properties for the Pittsburgh Penguins for over four years.

He is a two-time Emmy Award nominee and a recipient of a proclamation from the City of Pittsburgh. He was awarded a 2013 Golden Quill Award from the Press Club of Western Pennsylvania and has earned accolades from the Pennsylvania Association of Broadcasters and the US Harness Writers Association.

Mike has earned degrees from Dartmouth College, Yale University, and the University of Massachusetts at Amherst.

Connect with this Contributor

Scan this QR code to connect with Mike Lee on LinkedIn or visit http://www.studiousone.com.

Rick Landesberg is the principal of Landesberg Design, a design firm specializing in communications for higher education, philanthropic, and community-based clients with offices in Pittsburgh and New York City.

Rick was a founder and board member of the Pittsburgh chapter of the American Institute of Graphic Artists and has taught at the Carnegie Mellon University School of Design for over 15 years. Rick has also judged the Communication Arts Design annual competition and is active in several Pittsburgh cultural organizations.

In 2010, his work earned him the American Institute of Graphic Artists Fellow Award, which recognizes designers who have significantly impacted their local design community and AIGA chapter.

Connect with this Contributor

Scan this QR code to connect with Rick Landesberg on LinkedIn or visit http://www.landesbergdesign.com.

Michael Lotenero is the Principal and Creative Director at Michael Lotenero Art + Design where he has served a number of notable clients such as The Museum of Contemporary Art in San Diego, Nintendo, IBM, Sony Pictures, Panasonic, and Lowe's.

Michael has received accolades from several prestigious groups including The Addys, the American Institute of Graphic Artists, Graphic Design USA, and Graphis. He also earned The Award of Excellence from HOW Magazine in two categories and collaborated on a short film titled "Navarro" which documented his painting process.

He has been featured in dozens of solo and group exhibitions since earning his degree at the Art Institute of Pittsburgh in 1988.

Connect with this Contributor

Scan this QR code to connect with Michael Lotenero on LinkedIn or visit http://www.lotenero.com.

Saul Markowitz is the President of Markowitz Communications, a Pittsburgh-based marketing and public relations agency. Since 1997, the agency has prided itself on maximizing their "clients' media exposure while minimizing their expenditures."

Markowitz Communications has served such notable clients as AT&T, Cirque du Soleil, PetSmart, Krispy Kreme Doughnuts, and the Washington County Tourism and Promotion Agency.

Saul began his public relations career working with Pittsburgh icons such as the Pittsburgh Zoo, Carnegie Mellon University College of Fine Arts, and the Pittsburgh Symphony Orchestra.

Connect with this Contributor

Scan this QR code to connect with Saul Markowitz on LinkedIn or visit http://www.markowitzcommunications.com.

Dennis Moran is the President of Dennis Moran Design where he serves as Principal and approaches design as a strategic business tool. Since 1988, Dennis Moran Design has worked with large and small clients ranging from Highmark Blue Cross to technology start-ups.

Dennis also founded and served as Principal at Adam, Filippo & Moran for nine years and was an Adjunct Associate Professor of Design at Carnegie Mellon University.

He has been recognized by numerous national organizations including the American Institute of Graphic Arts, The New York and Chicago Art Directors Clubs, The Type Directors Club of New York, and Communication Arts Magazine.

Connect with this Contributor

Scan this QR code to connect with Dennis Moran on LinkedIn or visit http://www.morandesign.com.

Glenn Przyborski has acted as Director and Cinematographer at Przyborski Productions Inc., a television commercial production agency based in Pittsburgh, since 1988. The agency specializes in creating commercials to serve all audience sizes, from regional to network television.

He also has almost 15 years of experience developing commercial television campaigns prior to founding Przyborski Productions. Glenn worked with the Television Production Center Inc., where he was one of the pioneers in film post-production, and at Hartwick, Przyborski Productions which had offices in Pittsburgh, New York City, and Chicago.

Glenn's work has been recognized with numerous awards including Addys, Tellys, Emmys, and several regional "Best of Shows."

Connect with this Contributor

Scan this QR code to connect with Glenn Przyborski on LinkedIn or visit http://blog.przyborski.com.

Raelin Sawka Musuraca is a Customer Experience Strategist with over 20 years of experience in marketing, digital strategy, and user experience. Her cross-disciplinary education at Carnegie Mellon University and diverse professional experience has prepared her to approach marketing problems with a unique perspective.

Raelin is currently the Senior Customer Experience Strategist and Researcher at American Eagle Outfitters in Pittsburgh and has previously worked with several creative marketing agencies in Pittsburgh in leadership positions.

Throughout her career, she has provided services to several notable companies such as Supervalu, Proctor & Gamble, PPG Industries, PNC Financial Services, and GlaxoSmithKline.

Connect with this Contributor

Scan this QR code to connect with Raelin Musuraca on LinkedIn or visit http://musuraca.com.

Chauncey Smith is a healthcare marketing and business development professional with over 20 years of experience in B2B marketing and pharmaceutical marketing. Chauncey is the founder of MarketSMITH Services, LLC, a contract marketing and business development agency specializing in healthcare industries.

Chauncey previously worked in leadership roles at major healthcare organizations, such as GlaxoSmithKline Consumer Healthcare where he served as Senior Brand Manager for 10 years.

While at GlaxoSmithKline, his leadership was crucial in growing the CITRUCEL supplement brand from a $15 million asset in 1996 to a $70 million asset in 2001. He has also led marketing efforts with several other notable pharmaceutical products such as Abreva, Cutivate, and Aclovate.

Connect with this Contributor

Scan this QR code to connect with Chauncey Smith on LinkedIn or visit http://www.marketsmithservices.com.

Julie Smith has worked with RJW Media, a firm specializing in media planning and purchasing in Pittsburgh, since 1998. She currently serves as the President and Principal.

Julie began her career at local radio and television stations until she moved to the Dudreck, DePaul, Ficco, and Morgan Advertising firm where she spent 15 years and rose to the position of Senior Vice President, Director of Media. She later also became the Advertising Manager for SUPERVALU-Pittsburgh division.

She has been recognized several times by the Media Association of Pittsburgh. Julie earned the Best Overall Professional Award in 2001, 2002, 2003, and 2004 and was also awarded the Best Media Director/Supervisor Award in 2005.

Connect with this Contributor

Scan this QR code to connect with Julie Smith on LinkedIn.

David Sladack is currently the Senior Vice President, Group Account Director at Brunner, Inc., a top 75 US advertising agency with offices in Pittsburgh, Atlanta, and Washington D.C. At Brunner, Inc., he has worked with several notable brands including Ford, Cub Cadet, and Zippo.

He has previously worked in leadership and management positions at the St. George Group and St. John & Partners.

David has also served as an Adjunct Professor at Point Park University in Pittsburgh for over eight years and previously taught at Robert Morris University as an Adjunct Professor for nine years.

Connect with this Contributor

Scan this QR code to connect with David Sladack on LinkedIn or visit http://brunnerworks.com.

Jack Wolf is a freelance photographer who has established himself as one of Pittsburgh's most recommended photographers over the course of his 33-year career, shooting marquee sporting events such as Super Bowl XL, Super Bowl XLIII, Super Bowl XLV, and 18 USGA and PGA Tour events

Prior to picking up a camera at age 35, Jack enjoyed a seven-year career at Ketchum, MacLeod & Grove, an advertising firm based in Pittsburgh. After a friend introduced Jack to the world of photography, however, he left his job as an advertiser in pursuit of loftier ambitions as a freelance photographer.

While major awards have eluded Jack for the most part, he considers himself "big around the house" and notes a particular joy when cashing the checks for his projects. In addition, Jack despises hunting, fishing, and sailing, saying that these activities are "boring" and "senseless."

Connect with this Contributor

Scan this QR code to connect with Jack Wolf on LinkedIn or visit http://www.jackwolfphotography.com.

Rank does not confer privilege or give power. It imposes responsibility.

- Peter F. Drucker, American Management Consultant, Educator, and Author

Context | A Timeline of These 20 Years

To understand these 20 years in communications, it will help to remind those of us who were there what was going on in politics, culture and technology that impacted our world and the decisions we made.

For those of you who were not, this section will help provide some context for you to better understand the commentary throughout. This is not a history lesson, but a synopsis of what happened between 1990-2010 that shaped who we are, explains where we came from, and gives a glimpse of what happened along the way.

1990 | George H.W. Bush President of the United States, the fall of the Berlin Wall. Release of Nelson Mandela, Gulf War, Hubble Telescope launched into space, Photoshop 1.0 is released exclusively for Macintosh

1991 | Collapse of the Soviet Union, Los Angeles Police Officers indicted for videotaped beating of Rodney King, Tim Berners-Lee announces the World Wide Web project and the first website is created at info.cern.ch

1992 | End of the Cold War, Bosnian War begins, Sinéad O'Connor tears photo of Pope John Paul II on Saturday Night Live, the first SMS text message sent from a computer to a mobile phone

1993 | Bill Clinton President of the United States, Federal ATF agents raid Branch Davidian compound in Waco, TX leading to 51-day standoff, first SMS text message is sent from a mobile phone to another mobile phone

1994 | Rwanda Genocide, North American Free Trade Agreement goes into effect, Amazon.com is founded, Pizza Hut announces online orders, first banner ad appears on hotwired.com, Netscape is founded

1995 | First American astronaut rides in Soviet-launched Soyuz, Mississippi ratifies Thirteenth Amendment becoming the last state to abolish slavery, OJ Simpson Trial, DVD introduced as an optical disc storage format

1996 | Chess computer Deep Blue beats champion Garry Kasparov but loses rematch, successful cloning of the Dolly Sheep, Motorola introduces StarTac wearable cellular phone, Future Splash is acquired by Macromedia and released as Flash

1997 | Death of Princess Diana, 39 Heaven's Gate cultists commit suicide in California, Pathfinder sends back images of Mars, Netflix is founded, and Philippe Kahn is the first to share photos from a cell phone

1998 | US Senate approves Resolution 71 authorizing President Clinton to take action against Iraq, CBS telecasts *The Wizard of Oz* for the last time before cable gains rights, *Titanic* becomes most successful movie ever, Google is founded

1999 | Kosovo War, Euro is established, Bill Clinton acquitted in impeachment hearings, Chinese government restriction on Internet use in Internet cafes, ReplayTV and TiVo introduce DVR at the Consumer Electronics Show, BlackBerry releases the 850, Napster is released

2000 | New Zealand broadcasting on Chatham Island shared millennium celebration worldwide, Y2K Bug, Florida Election Recount, PlayStation released in Japan, *405 The Movie* first short film released on Internet, Microsoft ruled to have violated US antitrust laws, AOL and Time Warner merge

2001 | First tourist into space, No Child Left Behind Act passed, Sept. 11 Attacks, Apple launches the iPod and iTunes, BellSouth abandons the pay phone business due to competition with cell phones, Wikipedia launches

2002 | Golden Jubilee of Elizabeth II, Euro notes and coins introduced throughout Europe, Mars Odyssey space probe begins to map the surface of Mars, US invades Afghanistan, Iran bans American advertising

2003 | Gulf War II, Space Shuttle Columbia disintegrates during reentry, MySpace is founded, LinkedIn launches, WordPress is released, Apple releases Mac OS X Panther, Flash Mobs start in New York, Johnny Cash dies

2004 | NASA lands on Mars, Asia Tsunami, Taipei 101 opens as world's tallest skyscraper at 1,670 feet, Facebook launches, Google acquires Earth Viewer and later renames it Google Earth

2005 | George W. Bush re-elected to second term, Death of Pope John Paul II, Kuwaiti women granted right to vote, Hurricane Katrina, YouTube is founded, RadioHead releases *In Rainbows* in "pay what you want" format

2006 | Former Beatle Paul McCartney turns 64 after writing "When I'm 64" at the age of 16, North Korea conducts first nuclear test, Twitter is founded, Google acquires YouTube, WikiLeaks launches

2007 | Apple's Steve Jobs announces the first iPhone, *Harry Potter and the Deathly Hollows* sells 11 million copies in 24 hours, Hulu is founded, Writers Guild of America goes on strike, the Chunnel opens under the English channel providing train service from the UK to France

2008 | Mumbai attacks, election of President Obama, first Proton beam is circulated in collider at CERN, Petroleum hits $100 per barrel for the first time, Nokia sells more camera phones than Kodak sells film-based cameras

2009 | US and Russian satellites collide over Serbia, Somali pirates capture the cargo ship Maersk Alabama, H1N1 "swine flu" deemed global pandemic, Death of Michael Jackson

2010 | Greece receives €110 economic bailout, Haiti Earthquake, first 24-hour flight of a solar-powered plane, International Space Station exceeds record for longest human occupation in space, Apple releases the iPad, Pinterest is launched, WikiLeaks releases 250,000 American diplomatic documents

Kevin Popović and Rick Landesberg meeting on the set of *20YEARS Communications*. Photo courtesy of Jack Wolf.

Chapter 01 | Meet the Panelists

Introduction

Asking the question, "What do you do?" to a room full of communications professionals will yield dozens of different answers, yet it is an important question to ask. It provides some understanding of why they may answer later questions as they do and contributes to the baseline of this program i.e., "Who are these people, and why should I value their perspective?"

Communications is a broad field comprised of multiple channels. Though the specialists of each interact and often collaborate to accomplish a common objective, vertical isolation is not unusual. An aspiring designer will go to design school, affiliate with professional design associations like the American Institute of Graphic Arts (AIGA), and spend the rest of her career designing. An aspiring public relations professional will enroll in a public relations program, join the Public Relations Student Society of America (PRSSA), and network her way into a position at a PR agency or a PR department within an organization. The fields of advertising, production, and multimedia follow similar trajectories.

Even though professionals in communications segment themselves, they are connected by the ultimate goal of communicating effectively with an audience even if the medium, motivation, and strategy varies, which is why we interviewed experienced professionals from across the communications spectrum. We wanted to explore what they had in common and what was different.

None of us knows as much as all of us. A unified conversation covering the breadth of communication, like the one contained in this book, can be powerful. We can learn from the individuals working outside of our specialties so that we can not only expand our knowledge and improve our skills but also improve our ability to collaborate with experts from other disciplines. We can better understand their perspective, and they can better understand ours.

Perspective and Context

We are more than what we do. We are shaped by a sum of experiences both from within an industry and from without. Where we come from is just as important for understanding our perspectives as what we do. By asking our panelists how they began their careers—learning their motivations and their paths—we reveal an insight that is relevant for contextualizing their responses to later questions.

Whether a professional enjoys their job or not is important for understanding the answer. A disgruntled employee is likely to answer a question much differently than someone who is completely satisfied with their work and their work environment. For the later questions to have meaning, a reader must understand who is providing answers.

At the same time, career satisfaction is incredibly important and relevant, both for those of us working in communications and for those of us that are considering a career in the industry.

In 2010, when the interviews in this book were conducted, the Conference Board (Gibbons, 2010) conducted a survey of 5,000 households and found that only 45% of the respondents were satisfied with their jobs, a drop from 1987's 61.1%. With 55% of Americans unhappy with their career, one might expect our small sample to reflect that dissatisfaction to some degree, but it does not. Our participants, having spent over 20 years in their fields, were on the whole satisfied with their work and passionate about their careers. Admittedly, our sample is small, but the responses should still be encouraging for those interested in communications. But why are our panelists satisfied with their career choice?

Job security, according to the Society for Human Resource Management (2011), is the number one determinant of job satisfaction, but it is followed closely by the opportunity to use one's skills and abilities on the job. In an industry with a reputation of being fluid and sometimes unpredictable in terms of job security, the chance to use one's skills and abilities likely plays a significant role in the career satisfaction of our panelists, especially since many of them expressed a childhood fascination with creativity in the form of art or music or advertising. With careers in art and music being somewhat limited, perhaps we should not be surprised that communications professionals are satisfied to have a paying outlet for their creativity.

At the same time, many of our panelists are entrepreneurs. They own their businesses, either in freelance form or in the form of agencies or firms. Multiple studies suggest that entrepreneurs and professionals who choose to be self-employed are, on the whole, happier than those who choose traditional employment (Bidwell & Mollick, 2012; Binder & Coad, 2012). These same studies support the findings of the Society for Human Resource Management: autonomy and self-direction dramatically improve satisfaction. Having the freedom to work around family and work conflicts and having greater control over one's future results in a happier lifestyle.

Another contributing factor, which was revealed in a later discussion of technology's impact on how we communicate, may be the ability to telecommute as a communications professional. With the flattening of our world as Thomas Friedman (2007) describes it, the growing prevalence of telecommuting may impact career satisfaction in communications, especially since working from home is common for small business owners and freelancers. Global Workplace Analytics and the Telework Research Network released a report in 2011 that estimates that 20 to 30 million Americans are telecommuting, working from home at least once a week. Of that 30 million, an estimated 10 to 15 million are running a home business, 15 to 20 million (including the self-employed) work at home part time, and a total of 3 million are telecommuting full time. Telecommuting is becoming more and more common, increasing by 66% from 2005 to 2010.

We did not investigate how often our panelists telecommute, but we do know from our interviews that the ability to video conference and to transfer large files via the Internet has expanded the reach of agencies and improved collaboration both inside of an agency and between professionals separated by significant distance. Telecommuting is a part of the communications industry, and we suspect that it will continue to grow. In fact, researchers are already finding that teleworkers are happier with their jobs than office-based workers (Fonner & Roloff, 2010). If a worker telecommutes at least three days a week, the flexible work arrangement reduces work-life conflicts, lowers stress, and reduces the amount of distractions. The Internet has certainly been an increasingly important part of communications, so it may be that the integration of the Internet with communications is playing a role in the happiness of communications professionals alongside their ability to apply their passion to their work and to potentially own their own business.

Embarking on the 20 Years Journey

As you get to know the panelists in this book, and as we look back on the last 20 years and look ahead to the next 20 years, consider their backgrounds. Consider where they have come from, consider what they think of their work, and use that knowledge to create a greater context for their later answers. Also consider what you have learned about communications from your teachers, from your peers, from trade publications, and from professional experience. Your personal context is just as important as the context of the panelists, and answering our questions as you read the answers of our panelists will allow you to join the conversation and learn more about the field of communications and where you fit within it.

Q1 | What is your job in communications?

Kevin Popović: Founder of Ideahaus

I'm Kevin Popovic, and I am the founder of Ideahaus and the author of *Satellite Marketing*. I help my clients figure out what to say and how to say it.

Glenn Przyborski: Director/Cinematographer, Przyborski Productions

I'm Glenn Przyborski, and I direct and photograph TV commercials, so technically I'm a director, cinematographer. That's what I do.

Bill Flanagan: Executive Vice President, Corporate Relations, Allegheny Conference

My name is Bill Flanagan. I'm an Executive Vice President of Corporate Relations for the Allegheny Conference on Community Development and our affiliates: the Pittsburgh Regional Alliance, the Greater Pittsburgh Chamber of Commerce, and the Pennsylvania Economy League of South Western Pennsylvania. We do economic development. We work to make the region better, and we work to tell the world about it in hopes that people will invest here.

Julie Smith: Principal/President RJW Media

I'm Julie Smith, and I'm a Principal and President of RJW media. We're a full service media firm based in Pittsburgh, and we handle media planning and buying for our clients in all forms of media.

Brian Bronaugh: President/Executive Creative Director, Mullen – Pittsburgh

My name is Brian Bronaugh. I am the President and Executive Creative Director for the Pittsburgh office of Mullen. My primary job is to plant the flag every day for the agency. So my day is spent, for the most part, ringing the new business bell, conversing with folks in our office and with our clients, and making sure people believe in what we're doing.

Guido D'Elia: Partner, Mind Over Media

My name is Guido D'Elia, and I am a partner in Mind Over Media. I consult on strategy issues with companies and with clients to solve problems and move projects forward.

Chauncey Smith: Chief Sales and Marketing Director, ScienceMedia

I'm Chauncey Smith, and I'm the Chief Sales and Marketing Director for ScienceMedia. We're a small, independent shop that creates customized medical education sales training and communications.

Rob Deaner: Founder/Composer, Market Street Sound

I'm Rob Deaner, and I am a founder of Market Street Sound. I'm a composer, audio producer, music producer, and recording engineer. Anything in advertising that squeaks, honks, sings, or boinks—that's what we do all day.

Paige Beal: Assistant Professor, Marketing & Advertising, Point Park University

I'm Paige Beal. I'm an assistant professor in the Sport, Art, Entertainment Management program at Point Park University. I teach marketing and advertising and principally addressing it from a sport, art, entertainment management perspective.

Don Decker: Regional Sales, Comcast Spotlight

I am Don Decker, and I work for Comcast Spotlight, Regional Sales here in Pittsburgh which entails selling local and regional clients time on one of our 50+ cable networks.

Michael Hills: Vice President/General Manager, Comcast Spotlight

My name is Michael Hills. I'm the Vice President, General Manager for Comcast Spotlight, which is the television and Internet advertising branch of Comcast.

Rick Landesberg: Principal, Landesberg Design

My name is Rick Landesberg. I'm a graphic designer, and I have a design firm called Landesberg design. We've been in business for 28 years.

Mike Lee: Founder/Executive Producer, Studious One

My name is Mike Lee. I am a producer, writer, actor, director, etcetera—for myself and for a company that I have called Studious One.

Michael Lotenero: Designer/Artist, Michael Lotenero Art + Design

My name is Michael Lotenero. I am a painter, designer, illustrator, musician, dad–I'm pretty much whatever comes my way that day–that's pretty much what I do. That's the best way to put it, I guess.

Saul Markowitz: President, Markowitz Communications
My name is Saul Markowitz. I'm the president of Markowitz communications, and for the past 20 years I've volunteered to do PR. Actually, I don't get paid to do any of this stuff. I just do it for fun.

Dennis Moran: Principal, Dennis Moran Design
My name is Dennis Moran and I run my own business, a company called Dennis Moran Design. I've been running that since 1988. Our business is primarily strategic-level graphic design. I'm not trying to sound highfalutin about that but the actual work we do is strategic in nature.

Raelin Sawka Musuraca: Digital Strategist
I'm Raelin Sawka, and I'm a digital strategist. We work with our clients to determine what they want to achieve and then which digital technologies work best for them in that area. It may be web, it may be social media, or it may be banner ads, but something that's sort of living in the digital realm, not the traditional print or broadcast realm.

David Sladack: VP & Group Account Strategy Director, Brunner Advertising
I'm Dave Sladack. I'm the vice president and group account strategy rector at Brunner Advertising. My main responsibility is to handle the client relationships at a higher level and really just develop the brand strategy and kind of orchestrate the whole process.

Roy Cheran: Director of Business Development, Mind Over Media
Roy Cheran, Director of Business Development at Mind Over Media.

Jack Wolf: Commercial Photographer, Wolf Photography
My name is Jack Wolf and I currently am a commercial photographer.

I worked in an advertising agency. I was in television production. I was that actor in the first MTV video. I'm the author of line: "One for the Thumb." That was the biggest thing I'll ever do, and to top it off I'm going to end up as a messenger. Things come and go. That's the whole routine in the advertising world.

What do you do?

Q2 | How did you get into communications?

Guido D'Elia: Partner, Mind Over Media

By accident. I got into this business because I was exposed to it at a local station and got excited about being in production. I got excited that people could see your work. I got excited that there was some level of applause or recognition and had a big enough ego that it got me hooked.

Rob Deaner: Founder/Composer, Market Street Sound

I had been a musician my whole life, and like any musician I worked various jobs throughout high school and college—playing in a band at night, trying to succeed, but I didn't really like it. A friend of mine had gotten me into doing some music for a Hoover commercial out of Richmond, Virginia in the mid '80s, and that kind of opened my eyes. I thought, "Wow, how can I keep doing this?" So when I came back to Pittsburgh, I was looking around and keeping my ears open as to who was doing advertising and post-production. I found a post-production facility that had no audio department and wanted one. Foolishly, I had enough gear that I just said, "You know, why don't you just kind of give me a room here, and I will be your audio division?"

Kevin Popović: Founder of Ideahaus

My misspent youth of playing video games, skateboarding, painting band logos on the back of jean jackets and trying to make some sense of it all. My mother likes to say it was my spoiled inner child.

Glenn Przyborski: Director/Cinematographer, Przyborski Productions

I got into the business because my dad was one of the cameramen at Cape Kennedy. When you see those old rocket launches from History Channel, he was one of about 12 guys back in the early '60s and part of the '70s that used to photograph literally everything that got launched into space. It was kind of neat because I was always around these guys… they didn't call themselves filmmakers. They called themselves cameramen, but they had some great stories, and I thought, "That's an interesting job." I was always around cameras, so that's how I got involved in it.

Don Decker: Regional Sales, Comcast Spotlight

Initially, I had family members that were in the business when I was in high school, so I had a conversation with them about sales, about advertising sales and it sounded interesting, sounded fun. I had the chance to meet some neat people and clients and companies, so when I graduated from Duquesne University I started applying to jobs and talking to radio stations to get involved in advertising sales.

Michael Hills: Vice President/General Manager, Comcast Spotlight

I got into the business because my mother was a director for Greenbriar Treatment Centers. This was twenty some years ago, and part of her job was to do marketing and advertising for four or five Greenbriar Centers. At the time, I was interning at Communications, Inc., which was Blattner Brunner back then, and she had talked to me a little bit about how I ought to check this advertising sales thing out. She was talking a lot about her compadres who did that work for her at the different advertising mediums, and I met a lot of them. That's how I got here.

David Sladack: VP & Group Account Strategy Director, Brunner Advertising

My dad was a CPA, so I followed that suit, and it didn't take me very long to realize I didn't want to be an accounting major. I jumped into marketing, and I was fortunate enough to break into the Pittsburgh market as a media planner and buyer while I was working on my MBA. It was really a great foundation for really learning the overall business from a numbers standpoint, being a business major, and having that accounting experience. It was a great foundation for me to jump right into account service too.

Chauncey Smith: Chief Sales and Marketing Director, ScienceMedia

I spent a lot of years as a product manager, both here at GlaxoSmithKline and with Becton Dickinson as well, in the medical device industry. And a lot of years in sales. It was a natural progression from those pursuits.

Mike Lee: Founder/Executive Producer, Studious One

How'd I get into the business? You know what it was actually kind of that cliché story where you were discovered. It happened that way in front of the camera where an agent saw me and obviously was taken aback by my amazing looks and my muscular physique and thought, "You know…" No, but I started back in '97 just by accident in the job I was at in professional sports. I got into media production, so I was getting a little bit behind the scenes and a little bit in front of the camera. Eventually I put that together.

Bill Flanagan: Executive Vice President, Corporate Relations, Allegheny Conference

Well, through the back door. I worked as a TV reporter for most of the time. I've been in Pittsburgh for 20 years, and out of the blue one day I got a call as they were merging these economic organizations and they said, "We're looking for a communications guy, would you be interested?" And so I checked it out and it sounded like a really good opportunity. I'd been telling the Pittsburgh story as a reporter, and so I really viewed this as similar. I'm still telling the Pittsburgh story, but now it's a more direct purpose of improving the economy.

Julie Smith: Principal/President RJW Media
I started in 1978, all those years ago, on the broadcast side at WTAE. Then I spent five years there and then jumped over to the agency side. I spent 15 years with DDFM, a full service agency, the highest media biller at that time in the market, in Pittsburgh.

Michael Lotenero: Designer/Artist, Michael Lotenero Art + Design
The first memory I have of being in the business was when I was in fourth grade. I really wasn't in the business but it was my first sale. I was actually in class, and I was doing a drawing of Jaws and this kid bought it off of me for five bucks, and that was my first big art sale. I was hooked. I was like, "this is it." So I think that was probably my first thing, my first step into the business.

Paige Beal: Assistant Professor, Marketing & Advertising, Point Park University
I was a double major undergraduate in psychology and sociology, which meant either going to school for the rest of my life or I could be a country radio DJ, so I went to work for a country radio station and that started about 30 years of multiple media exposures, from radio to TV to cable to Internet to newspaper, a little bit of everything.

Roy Cheran: Director of Business Development, Mind Over Media
I was a junior in high school, McKeesport Area Senior High School, and we had a visitor to our class one day. It was a television crew from Channel 11. I was so intrigued with the activity, the excitement, the lights, camera, action aspect of it. I said, "You know what? That's what I want to do when I grow up." And that's how I got in the business.

Rick Landesberg: Principal, Landesberg Design
I was an art kid, and it's unbelievable the number of classes I got out of in junior high school and high school so I could go do the Christmas mural. When I went to college, I was a painting major. I don't tell all my clients that, but that in fact was what I was. When I got out of school, I discovered that graphic design was a discipline. I always thought it was like advertising, and I was not interested in that. I had an anti-establishment root, but I started to realize that things like typography and design and things like that were a subject. I started to read about it, and I started to eat it up. I had actually gotten a very good design education in college but didn't know it.

Saul Markowitz: President, Markowitz Communications

I was working at the University of Pittsburgh (Pitt) radio station for a while, and I wrote for the Pitt News. Actually, the real story behind that is I'm the youngest of six boys, and we had no money. We were broke. I didn't realize we were broke, but we didn't have much going. When I went to college, I had to go to a state school so I could afford to go, and I realized if I become a promotions director at a radio station I could get all this free stuff. And what's so funny about this is I'm still doing it. It's so great.

Dennis Moran: Principal, Dennis Moran Design

Sister Fabian, my sixth grade teacher, is really responsible for that. I had a nun that recognized that I had artistic talent and that really became the incentive to study, first to study art then to study design. So, I studied at the Ivy School of Professional Art in Pittsburgh, a great school that's no longer around. Then I also studied at Carnegie Mellon University in Pittsburgh.

Raelin Sawka Musuraca: Digital Strategist

Writing and technology. I love to write, and as I was doing that, I found that I just understood technology. I had the ability to be able to communicate with people who were programmers or people that you might call the techy-geeky people. I could talk with them and communicate with them yet translate that for the rest of us and for the others. With a career in writing, it's really kind of difficult to make a living with that, but being able to combine the two I was able to do what I love and also be on the cutting edge of things, following new technologies and following new digital practices.

Brian Bronaugh: President/Executive Creative Director, Mullen – Pittsburgh

After attending Penn State University for four years and then Portfolio Center, a school in Atlanta, which I was drawn to because it guaranteed a job at the end of a two-year curriculum, I got my first internship. I interviewed anywhere and everywhere, but Ketchum at the time in Pittsburgh offered me a job for $12,500, thank you very much, and that was the best offer I had financially. Being newly married and a father of a one year old, it was time to go for a good opportunity with Ketchum to start my career.

Jack Wolf: Commercial Photographer, Wolf Photography

I graduated from college with a journalism degree and a minor in advertising. At that time, back when things were archaic but normal, you could actually go for a job at a firm where the people who work there actually work there. It was an advertising agency that had employees, and they had an internship. I was lucky enough to get one after I graduated. I started at 6-6-66. That was the day I started. With all the sixes, that's like bad luck right?

Q3 | Do you like working in communications?

Guido D'Elia: Partner, Mind Over Media

I like what I do. Looking back on it, there's been a lot of thrills, a lot of ups and downs, a lot of struggles, a lot of hard work, but a lot of fun. I've worked with some great people.

Glenn Przyborski: Director/Cinematographer, Przyborski Productions

I like what I do a lot. Yeah.

Saul Markowitz: President, Markowitz Communications

Yeah, actually I do. I've been doing it since 1985. I think it's a great field to get into and I'm very fortunate.

David Sladack: VP & Group Account Strategy Director, Brunner Advertising

I do. This is really a people-oriented business, and it gives you an opportunity to meet a whole bunch of different people. It also gives you an opportunity to really play in a lot of different industries and learn an awful lot about a lot of different things.

Don Decker: Regional Sales, Comcast Spotlight
Yeah, very much.

Rick Landesberg: Principal, Landesberg Design
On most days, I like what I do. There are certain things that come with the territory and those things are difficult, and those things will always be there. There will always be budgets. There will always be deadlines. There will always be some degree of bad behavior. However, the root of what it's about I like enormously. There is something about the design process, that kind of problem solving, which is fascinating.

Chauncey Smith: Chief Sales and Marketing Director, ScienceMedia
For the most part, I like what I do. It's a little bipolar. Some days I love it, some days I hate it, but for the most part, being able to work with the companies I get to work with and develop innovative solutions is both rewarding and a lot of fun.

Raelin Sawka Musuraca: Digital Strategist
I like what I do some days, and I don't like what I do other days. The most difficult thing being in communications is you can't necessarily always pick and choose the work that you work on.

Jack Wolf: Commercial Photographer, Wolf Photography
Now? Oh, I always did. Anybody that tells you photography is work is full of shit. You're taking pictures for God's sake. Work is when you lift something. If you lift things for a living, that's work. So I've never worked, and I've always been lucky. I'm very grateful for that because most people can't say that.

Bill Flanagan: Executive Vice President, Corporate Relations, Allegheny Conference
Yeah, it's fun. The fun part about working for the Allegheny County Conference and these organizations is that we do what news organizations do. You go around and you look for what's wrong, but the difference is if you're a reporter you go on the evening news that night and you say here's what's wrong somebody ought to do something. The nice part about working for the Allegheny Conference is that we work to fix it. So we look for problems, we develop solutions, and then we try to convince—more often than not—government to do something about it.

Brian Bronaugh: President/Executive Creative Director, Mullen – Pittsburgh
Yeah, I would say if I gave a percentage it was probably 80 to 90%. I really

do enjoy coming to work every day. It's not punching a time clock. There are certainly roller coaster kinds of emotions that happen. When you are told by a client that they're no longer going to work with you, or if you have to let somebody go, either for cause or economic reasons, those are days that are truly not enjoyable. But the pros far outweigh the cons, and I can't imagine having done anything else as a career right now

Kevin Popović: Founder of Ideahaus

I love what I do. I do what I used to run home from school to do for free, and I figured out how to get clients to cut me checks for it.

Roy Cheran: Director of Business Development, Mind Over Media

I love what I do. I think the primary reason that I like what I do is I've always liked interacting with people and building relationships with people. That should be an intrinsic component of what we do as partners with clients. The other thing that I like is the evolution of technology and the application of technology merging with the right strategy to help a client deliver their message effectively.

Mike Lee: Founder/Executive Producer, Studious One

I love what I do. I think there's nothing like doing what you want to do.

Paige Beal: Assistant Professor, Marketing & Advertising, Point Park University

I love what I do. I love teaching, but I also keep a foot in the door of the business world because I consult.

Julie Smith: Principal/President RJW Media
I love what I do. I love media, all aspects of it. I love making clients successful.

Michael Hills: Vice President/General Manager, Comcast Spotlight

I love it. Advertising is an interesting blend of art and science. I'm a creative person, so I love the artistic side of it, but there's a lot of science around how to make advertising work for customers. I enjoy helping businesses and people do great things through advertising.

Michael Lotenero: Designer/Artist, Michael Lotenero Art + Design
Yeah, I love what I do.

Dennis Moran: Principal, Dennis Moran Design
You know, I do love what I do. I won't say that there aren't times when I'm incredibly frustrated with it and hate parts of it, but I absolutely love the work.

Rob Deaner: Founder/Composer, Market Street Sound
I love what I do. First of all, I don't have to pour concrete today. I might tomorrow; you never know. A musician's life is always a bit of a roller coaster, but every day I get to come in and make something out of the air. That's really cool.

Discussion Questions

Review these questions in your head, or write them down to really think through your answer. Doing so now will help you process what you've just learned and enable you to apply this in the future.

1. What part of the communications industry do you work within, and how did you get there?

2. What influenced your decision to work within the field of communications?

3. What can you do differently that would improve your career satisfaction?

4. What are your perceptions of the different types of communications, and why?

5. Do you think a professional should be an expert in a single channel of communications, or should they be proficient in multiple channels? Explain your answer.

6. If you could choose, would you prefer working on the agency side (serving clients) or the client side (working for the business)? Why?

7. What responses surprised you the most, and why?

Join the Conversation

Scan the QR codes from this section to watch the video for each question, then read the comments shared by others in our community. Add your thoughts to join our conversation.

Q1 | What is your job in communications?

Q2 | How did you get into communications?

Q3 | Do you like working in communications?

There are four ways, and only four ways, in which we have contact with the world. We are evaluated and classified by these four contacts: what we do, how we look, what we say, and how we say it.

- Dale Carnegie, American Author, Lecturer

Kevin Popović and Glenn Przyborski discuss production on the set of *20YEARS*. Photo courtesy of Jack Wolf.

Chapter 02 | Communications

Introduction

The Sender and Receiver model of communication is day one for most introductory communications courses and rightly so. This model is the foundation of most modern communications research and provides a common understanding for professionals of every discipline within. In its most simplified form, as many will agree, whether you are selling services on the phone, marketing products with a television advertisement, or posting a link on a social network, communications is about delivering a message to a recipient. You have information that you want to transfer, via some form of channel, to someone else. It's sent, and it's received. If this model sounds mechanical, it should, as it was originally published in the book The Mathematical Theory of Communication (Shannon & Weaver, 1949) and focused mostly on how messages were transferred via radio, from one party to another.

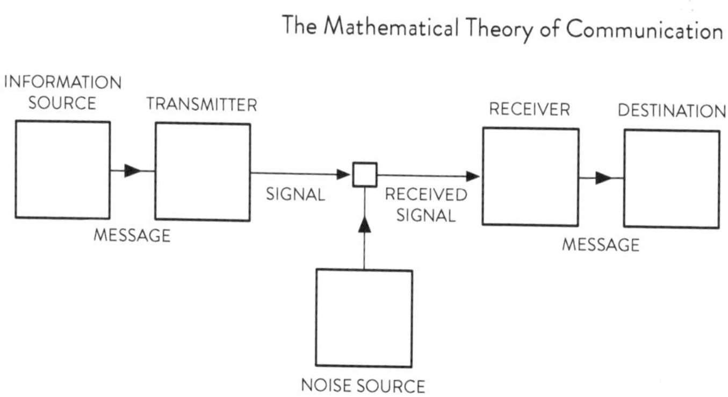

Fig. 1 – Schematic diagram of a general communication system.

Some 50 years later, the Sender and Receiver model has been revised and expanded dozens of times, each incarnation addressing a new nuance in communication or accounting for a growing complexity in contemporary communications. These later models talk about message encoding and decoding, about syntax, about semantics, about pragmatism, and a number of other variables and factors that might influence the communication process.

Represented visually, contemporary diagrams are often now a swirling mass of boxes, lines and arrows, detailing new thinking on how we communicate to more people with more media.

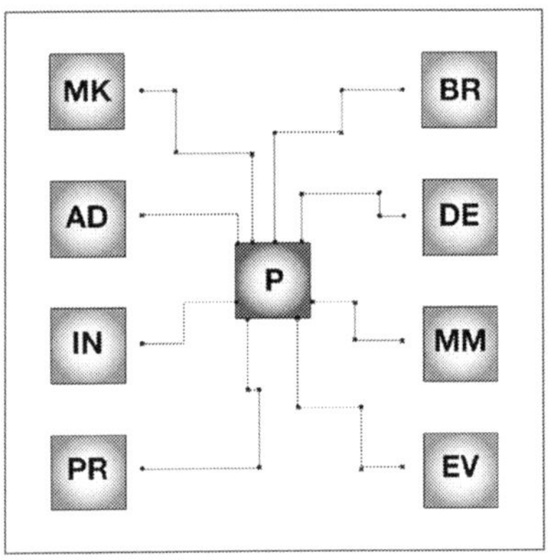

Conventional Marketing

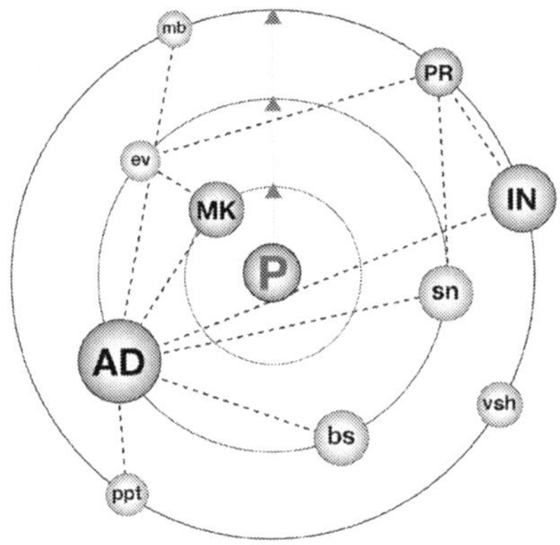

Satellite Marketing®

Communications in Practice

Scholarly research on communications is important, but how does that research translate to a professional setting? How do communication professionals define communications, if at all? And then, how does that definition impact their process? How do their respective processes intersect with each other, especially when serving the same client?

These questions may be difficult to answer for those of us who are new to communications, but our panelists have spent at least 20 years working in the industry. They have had time to test, retest, and revise their perspectives on communications and their approach to the process – their success and livelihood has counted on it. We were curious to see where the art of communications intersected with the science of communications and how our panelists reconciled the two in their work, especially after a long career in the field.

The definition of process, in the world of communications, can be frustratingly amorphous or rigidly concrete. At one end of the pendulum swing is Michelangelo seeing an angel in a block of marble and simply setting her free with his chisel and hammer, and at the other end is an approach as prescriptive as Carnegie's "*How to Win Friends and Influence People*." Neither would seem to be practical for a student new to communications or to a seasoned professional working with a diverse collection of clients and projects. The true goal of this discussion of process is to distill what is unique, what is the same, what is practical, and what point of the pendulum swing is most useful and effective.

Our panelists are most qualified to speak to this, both because of their experience and the range of disciplines that they represent.

The Human Element

In their discussion of process, many of our panelists emphasize the importance of audience, the importance of considering the people on the other end of the communications, how they think, what they care about, how they might interpret a message. As communications professionals, our work is constantly influenced by people: colleagues, clients, vendors, support staff, media. Our audience influences us. And the people in our lives, even if they come from outside of our professional life, influence us. For this reason, we asked our panelists what was the single biggest influence in their work, and though we left the question open to include answers other than people, most identified a person or a group of people that affected their outlook on communications and life.

The research and an overwhelmingly large body of anecdotal evidence points strongly to the positive effect that a mentor can have on an individual. Studies suggest that being mentored results in increased short-term career development and in psychosocial support, which translates to a growth in knowledge and greater psychosocial support in the future (D'Abete, 2010; Schatz, 1999; Hays & Minichiello, 2000; Givens, 2009). The one-on-one guidance of a mentor increases motivation, performance, and the likelihood of future success. As technology has advanced, the importance of having a mentor has not diminished, and there is no indication that this will change in the future.

Finding a mentor can be a difficult task, which is where networking comes into play. In communications, an industry largely comprised of short-term contracts and a revolving door of clients, networking can be the key to keeping the lights on. So not only is networking a proven factor in finding a job, it is a factor in keeping a job (Wolf & Moser, 2008).

We Are Never Not Communicating

The human element is ever-present at all points in communications, We are always communicating with someone, sending and receiving, encoding and decoding. Based on the research and our panelists' response, there is great benefit to paying attention and to communicating purposefully at every stage of our career and at every stage of our process.

Q4 | How do you define "communications"?

Kevin Popović: Founder of Ideahaus
I think in the simplest form it's a message between two people.

The textbook answer is a process between a sender and a receiver: a message is coded from the sender, it's decoded by the receiver, and it's interpreted. The process repeats from the other direction and - presto! - communication happens.

Glenn Przyborski: Director/Cinematographer, Przyborski Productions
Communications is the concept of one person trying to share his ideas with another person, or it could be a company trying to convey their ideas to an individual or another company.

Mike Lee: Founder/Executive Producer, Studious One
I define it as the transfer of a thought or idea from one person to the next.

Don Decker: Regional Sales, Comcast Spotlight
I define communications as a dialogue between one or two different parties, whether that dialogue is spoken, written, or gestured.

Chauncey Smith: Chief Sales and Marketing Director, ScienceMedia

Communications is a two-way process that occurs between a sender and a receiver, and there's a channel that connects the two of them.

Paige Beal: Assistant Professor, Marketing & Advertising, Point Park University

It's a very professorial perspective: the diagrams with the sender who encodes the message—that hopefully emerges throughout the noise of everything else—going on to the receiver, who then decodes the message from their perspective and gives feedback. I think of that as an application both for an interpersonal perspective as well as for a company to consumer or B2B or B2C, whatever it might be, perspective.

Guido D'Elia: Partner, Mind Over Media

I always try to look at things from the user's point of view and from the other person's point of view. Unless you understand your audience and their point of view—what they are looking for, what their needs are, what they've heard, what they haven't heard, what their perceptions might be on the subject you are talking about—you really can't communicate to them. You have to have those considerations, and I think that your results have to be based on their perception, not your perception of you or your message. It's that simple.

Rob Deaner: Founder/Composer, Market Street Sound

That's what music is, communication. For me, communication has to happen two ways: from one person to another, or one person to a group, and back. Communication comes from an idea and an action and a response. Rinse and repeat.

Julie Smith: Principal/President RJW Media

I think there's a two-pronged approach to communicating. The first one would be a more one-way communication, like with traditional media, and the second way would be more two-way, a more personal way, with the Internet and social media like Twitter or Facebook.

Dennis Moran: Principal, Dennis Moran Design

First of all, I think of it in its most simplistic form: it's a sender and a receiver. It's information that's moving between those two. Many, many people work in many different forms of communications, but at its heart that's really what it's about. Communications is about the transfer of information between a sender and receiver. Keep that in mind, but also realize that we're dealing with human beings here. Humans should be at the center of what we do, and the more we can understand those particular humans that we're trying to talk to the better we can do our job.

Michael Lotenero: Designer/Artist, Michael Lotenero Art + Design

I think that communicating accurately is a tough thing. It goes back to listening to the client and figuring out what the right way to say something is, how to say it, and where to say it. Understand your objective. Get to the essence of what the real problem is in communicating, and get that right the first time as opposed to wasting a lot of time and money.

Bill Flanagan: Executive Vice President, Corporate Relations, Allegheny Conference

What I always felt since I've been in the reporting business is that the first part of it is listening. What makes you a good communicator in the beginning is that you pay attention to what other people are saying. You try to digest that and understand where they're coming from and then that's going to put you in a much better position as a communicator to be able to tell the story.

Saul Markowitz: President, Markowitz Communications

I think of communications as telling a story and how you tell that story. How do I tell that story? Remember it's always the truth. You get your story by telling the truth, so it's our story and not somebody else's story.

Michael Hills: Vice President/General Manager, Comcast Spotlight

Communications is a broad, sweeping term, kind of like marketing. I would say that marketing is a big piece of communications, but if you had to define what is communications it is again the art and science of a business telling a story for the sake of getting some sort of action.

Raelin Sawka Musuraca: Digital Strategist

I learned the art of rhetoric, which to me is communications, which is getting someone to do or think the way that I want them to. Basically, I'm exerting an influence to achieve what I want. That may be selling a product. It may be raising money for a charity. It may be changing a political opinion, but in essence, every time I approach a project, I need to ask, "what do I want the target audience or person to do?" Communicating is that process.

David Sladack: VP & Group Account Strategy Director, Brunner Advertising

I look at it from a consumer decision-making standpoint. And in my opinion, it's our job to really take a look at each stage of that process and find ways that we cannot only influence each of those stages but also, especially in today's world with technology, find ways of developing that dialogue with a customer all the way through the process. From the time they realize that there's a need for a product—and we're trying to create and develop awareness— all the way through the post-purchase when we are trying to build their loyalty and turn them into an advocate.

Brian Bronaugh: President/Executive Creative Director, Mullen – Pittsburgh
I'm sure there are as many answers as people you're interviewing, and my definition would be: any and all touch points that we have with the people we're trying to communicate with. Touch point is to me a very broad definition of any intersection we have with our consumer, with our target, and that can come in a whole ecosystem of channels.

Roy Cheran: Director of Business Development, Mind Over Media
I think the best way to define communications is to put the word effective in front of it, because if it isn't effective, in my mind, it isn't communications. The key is to develop the right message from a strategic standpoint and to then look at the appropriate medium or mediums to communicate through and with, whether it's one-way or two-way.

Rick Landesberg: Principal, Landesberg Design
I'm a great believer in a line which I did not make up. There's a wonderful designer named Eric Speakerman who founded Meta Design, and he came up with a great line that I use all the time. That line is: you cannot not communicate. People are always communicating. Organizations are always communicating. The idea is that - can you understand and control that message. But that fact is something that's happening all the time, whether you try or not.

Jack Wolf: Commercial Photographer, Wolf Photography
When you talk to other people, when you tell them what you do, how you communicate to them, you get the word out where you work, where you live, how to get a hold of you—that's communications. So if anyone's in need of a photographer that used to work in advertising, right here. You have to tell people what you do. Hi, I'm Jack Wolf. I do photography.

Q5 | What is your process for communicating?

Raelin Sawka Musuraca: Digital Strategist
Everyone has a process. Everybody has their steps—ten, eight, twelve—but really what it comes down to is putting yourself in the shoes of your target audience. You really need to understand what is going to impact them, and you really need to understand that it all comes to a need. I may

be doing business to business communications. I may be writing sales flyers, but I'm still going to think about that person reading that flyer. What do they need? What can I say that's going to get them to react and to call the company I'm working for?

Brian Bronaugh: President/Executive Creative Director, Mullen – Pittsburgh

Sure, what agency wouldn't come in and say, "We've got our process and this is how we do things"?

I think that everything for us, and this isn't necessarily a unique thing, starts with understanding who it is we're talking to. We've invested heavily in the account planning side of the coin for the agency, and that means the way the target is walking, talking, breathing, living—we want to understand every facet of that so that messaging does intersect with them, and it's doing so in a relevant, authentic way that means something to them.

Chauncey Smith: Chief Sales and Marketing Director, ScienceMedia

Most of my communication at ScienceMedia is in the vein of business development, so yes, there is a pretty systematic process that I follow in terms of identifying the segment, what's going to be relevant to them, and based on a database that I've built over time certainly what would be elements or communication components that would be interesting to them. In most cases, you are trying to generate some initial interest or awareness, so we spend a lot of time on the prospecting end of communications.

Don Decker: Regional Sales, Comcast Spotlight

I probably come to format myself and my business day. That format is made up of e-mail, voicemail, faxes, telephone calls, and in-person calls, communicating directly live, so it's a combination of all things. It's kind of a smörgåsbord of those different techniques that work for my business.

Roy Cheran: Director of Business Development, Mind Over Media

The key to any level of success in our business, whether from an individual standpoint or from a company standpoint, is you have to quickly differentiate yourself from the pack because I don't think people want to be bored and bothered with too many "me-toos."

Rob Deaner: Founder/Composer, Market Street Sound

My process is to learn as much about the situation as quickly as possible and to approach it with an open mind. I don't come in with the notion that I know what to do right away. I let the project tell me as much as it can about what to do, and then I go from there because each project has unique specifics. For me, the creativity in music and in sound happens in a very quick second. And then after that idea has been born, the rest of it is the craft and turning that idea an action.

As a musician, as a composer, I spend a couple of hours every day listening to music, finding new music, finding new uses for music. I ask myself, where is it being used? How is it being used? How, if it's commercial or a movie or an image-related music piece, is it relating? How is it helping propel the image or helping to magnify or convey the emotion? If it's not done well, what's getting in the way of the communication?

Guido D'Elia: Partner, Mind Over Media
I can't go anywhere unless I'm real clear on the target, and I'm real clear on the objective or the challenge. I can't start with any road or path or suggestions or recommendation until that's really solid. The build doesn't matter; it's the plan. The process is about identifying the need first, and unless that's done I just can't go there.

I need to start with what that client need is, what the audience is, what the need is at that point. Let's do enough research, let's do enough thinking, let's do enough probing so that we understand what it is we need to do. Even if it's done in advance, and someone lays it out and says here is exactly what we need, I have to challenge that somewhat just to be sure that I get it and I understand it and that everyone is in agreement with it.

Bill Flanagan: Executive Vice President, Corporate Relations, Allegheny Conference
At the end of the day, you really have to understand who you're trying to talk to and what you want them to do, and that's usually the first question I'll ask of anybody. What are you trying to get done and who are you trying to influence? And that becomes the beginning of everything we do, and I think I've learned that along the way. All good communication starts with a strong understanding of who you're trying to communicate with, who your target audience is. If you don't understand that or know that going in, you're going to waste enormous amounts of time and money and be ineffective no matter what.

Michael Hills: Vice President/General Manager, Comcast Spotlight
I tend to meet with my different departments, my advertising departments, sales, etcetera. Face-to-face is really the best way to communicate direction and most importantly to get feedback on what the direction should be. I don't use email for communication. I use email for distribution of information. It's a powerful tool, but it cannot replace face to face discussion or a phone call.

Rick Landesberg: Principal, Landesberg Design
In design, no matter what you're doing, no matter what the problem is, no matter who the client is, there's a mantra, a question. That core

question that should be asked, whether you're redesigning a museum or redesigning your plumber's business card, is: what is it really about?

A project always has to start with that question, and if there's a consensus on the answer then you have something to work with. That becomes the benchmark. That's the thing when you get lost you always come back to.

Mike Lee: Founder/Executive Producer, Studious One

The process starts with who your audience is, who you are, and the medium you're going to use. You have to consider all three throughout the process.

As important as it is to try to anticipate who your audience is, it's very subjective. And I try to look from the easy side first, somebody who's already in that camp. What's their take away from the message? And someone who's categorically opposed, on the other side—if they're receiving this message, what is their takeaway? You try to balance that. You can't please everybody. It's not going to work on everybody, but you certainly want to deal with that range and know what range you're dealing with before you create a message.

Michael Lotenero: Designer/Artist, Michael Lotenero Art + Design

It's hard for me to get in the right frame of mind if everything's not the way it needs to be before I start. All the tools have to be in the right place. It's this weird procrastination thing. You sort of walk around and get stupid things done, like all the dishes have to be clean around the house. The key for me is I try to paint every day. Whether it's some little small thing or something big doesn't matter, but to be in the studio every day and to do something is important to me.

Dennis Moran: Principal, Dennis Moran Design
There are jobs that are different, and the process would really depend on the scope of what you've been asked to do. I think there are some basic things that are common to just about any part of the design process, and I'm making a distinction about design. Design is not this decoration or arrangement of objects. Design, to me, is this intellectual process, and it's a big process in that it encounters many, many, many different disciplines: architecture, interior design, industrial design, product design, interior design, and graphic design.

Design disciplines share a common set of processes. Although people call them different things, and we use different words to define them, the process we use in almost anything is first about understanding and discovery. It's hard to do anything if you don't know the framework, so the first step in doing anything is to try to understand who you're trying to talk to, what their particular bias situation might be. Again you're getting at the heart of what we as humans are about.

The second phase is ideation. You develop alternatives, options, ideas. The third phase is taking those ideas and showing them to people, letting them react. You're weighing the options. You decide the good and the bad, and you deal with all of the things that might affect the message—the political and economic situation, the reality of what can be done, what's practical,what's possible. Then you test it, and implement it.

Paige Beal: Assistant Professor, Marketing & Advertising, Point Park University
It depends on who you are communicating with and the type of message involved. That's a critical key. You take that framework and dump into it the message and who is sending it and who is receiving it. That all fluctuates dramatically depending on those elements.

Glenn Przyborski: Director/Cinematographer, Przyborski Productions
I'm probably too logical. I would say that communicating with companies is like trying to imagine I'm that other person and what I would want to have told to me or something like that. That's the way I would logically go about thinking about it.

I remember once we had a company that was trying to call on us to do post-production. They sent over a thing that when you opened it up, it blew out all this confetti into your face, which ended up all over the floor and everything. I thought, "Boy, that's a really dumb thing." They did get our attention, but they didn't get any business because I didn't see any reason for it. They didn't think about being the other person.

David Sladack: VP & Group Account Strategy Director, Brunner Advertising
At the end of the day, it really is about following a decision making process. If it's the consumer decision-making process, I think we all know what that's about.

It starts with the consumer recognizing a need. Sometimes we create the need or help create the need. You generate awareness. You help the customer search through their alternatives and evaluate their alternatives by influencing them, by building conviction through the brand and educating and engaging them. You continue influencing them all the way through the persuasion process when the customer is about to make that purchase. And then of course afterward you offer some sort of post-purchase communication, a follow-up that tries to convert those folks into loyalists. And it works the same way with business. It's all about fulfilling and motivating a need.

Julie Smith: Principal/President RJW Media
We try to build long-term relationships with our clients as well as the media community because we're bringing the two together with a bridge. We're trying to bridge the two together for the common goal of meeting the client's objectives. We try to keep those strong relationships going and we also strive very hard to teach clients, to lead clients to learn our business because it's a two-way street. We try to learn as much as we can so that we can make the best decisions for our clients and in turn we feel they need to learn our business as well.

Jack Wolf: Commercial Photographer, Wolf Photography
Preproduction. The key to any good photo session is preproduction.

In other words, clients come to you and say, "We want you to do this to-morrow or the next week and it's down there on the South Side. It's going to be shot in this room and you'll be fine and they'll be this person." I go there the next day and I find out where I'm going to park and how I'm going to get into the building and what the lighting looks like and who the people are that are going to be there. I know all this before I'm going in, and then when I get there for the shoot, I'm smarter than anybody there. I know it before you do because I know exactly what we're going to do because I'm going to do it. I think that's a form of the communications process. Preproduction. Key.

Kevin Popović: Founder of Ideahaus

I'm a process guy. I've got a process for just about everything. I don't know if that's part of my ADD, obsessive compulsive side, which has served me well because of my process.

I've got a process planning our client's communications, I've got a process to plan a web site. I've got a process for when I develop advertising or corporate identities or social media. The process, I think, provides a foundation for us to be creative and experimental yet keep us on track and on budget.

I'm suspect of someone without a process, you know what I mean? Are you going to wing this? I don't think so.

Q6 | What has been the single biggest influence in how you communicate?

Glenn Przyborski: Director/Cinematographer, Przyborski Productions

The single biggest influence, I would say, is the invention of the computer because of how integrated that is and the way we work today compared to years ago. Years ago I wouldn't have said that. I would have said watching movies or watching other TV shows would be how you were influenced, but today I think half the stuff we do would be almost impossible without computers.

Raelin Sawka Musuraca: Digital Strategist

I had two professors that were in very different disciplines: Dan Borowski in the graphic design department and Dave Kauffer in the writing program. They were sort of on the edge, and they encouraged me to pursue both disciplines and combine them.

Michael Hills: Vice President/General Manager, Comcast Spotlight

I use a personal coach and have for about five years in terms of helping me be a better leader and a better communicator. She's changed my entire life and my approach to business and people.

Chauncey Smith: Chief Sales and Marketing Director, ScienceMedia

The single biggest influence is probably a real belief in that communication, and how you develop it can be both systematic and creative. The creativity gets a chance to break through when you've got set milestones in how you like to develop things.

Paige Beal: Assistant Professor, Marketing & Advertising, Point Park University

I think my own form of ADD has been the biggest influence, and I'm very fortunate for that because I've always looked for change. I get bored quite easily, and I think that enabled me to adopt a variety of different media experiences and to look for the next envelope.

Kevin Popović: Founder of Ideahaus

I've got to say my biggest influence is probably my father, Dr. Charles Popovich, a marketing professor and business consultant, and someone who always helped me keep in mind those marketing basics. Those marketing basics have helped keep my creative guy in check. Having a mix of those two has probably served my clients well.

Rick Landesberg: Principal, Landesberg Design

My parents had a big influence on me, particularly my father. They were inquisitive, and they were curious. That is one of the great things about what design invites one to do. It invites one to be quite curious and inquisitive about the world.

My father went into business for himself in his 50s. I was in college, and he was in the steel mill equipment business, hardball stuff. Real hard-assed, wheeler dealer stuff. He had worked for a big company, and it was a great risk for him at that age. I remember he said two things to himself, and I still think it's good advice to anyone who goes into business for themselves today. He said, "My typewriter has the same number of keys as everybody else's, and my phone calls every other phone." Good advice.

Mike Lee: Founder/Executive Producer, Studious One

I think it's partly because I was raised the way I was, to be broad ranged and well-rounded to get me into a good school, a good college. I kept it going for the rest of my life, so I tend to be very curious about different aspects of whatever it is I'm doing. I think that's valuable, and for me it's very valuable to understand enough to be dangerous.

Michael Lotenero: Designer/Artist, Michael Lotenero Art + Design

It's hard to put a finger on all of the different influences, and a lot of my influences are the people around me. My grandfather influenced my work ethic. That definitely comes to mind. And my kids, definitely. Having kids changed everything for me in terms of how I do things, why I do things, and really making sure that I play every day and have a good time with them.

Roy Cheran: Director of Business Development, Mind Over Media

The single biggest influence for me in doing what I do and the way I do it was probably my mom. The character she always demonstrated, the approachability, the frankness and honesty, and the fun and humor she brought to everything are some of the characteristics that fortunately rubbed off on me. Those qualities have molded me as a person and my personality and the way I interact with people.

Saul Markowitz: President, Markowitz Communications

I love working with people who are better than I am. I have this thing about that. I look at my career, and I'm very, very lucky.

David Sladack: VP & Group Account Strategy Director, Brunner Advertising

It really is a people business, and I've been fortunate to have been associated with many smart and dynamic people. I think the one that stands out in my mind is Herb Burger. Herb Burger is an old titan in this industry in Pittsburgh, and boy, the guy just really knew how to get things done. He took me under his wing and is still a mentor of mine today.

Dennis Moran: Principal, Dennis Moran Design

There's probably more than one, and it's probably both people and other organizations, certainly tons of people. There were two really influential people who were mentors to me. One was a professor at Carnegie Mellon and also a really accomplished Pittsburgh advertising professional, a guy named Fran Esteban. He taught senior design, and then I worked with him at a company called Aubrey Lee Associates in Pittsburgh. Another mentor on that same level was a guy by the name of Don Grape. He was a design director at my first job, a company called Creative Productions in Pittsburgh.

There are these posters where they show the origins of members of rock groups, where they show this interconnection. It looks like everyone descends from the same group of bands. It's strange, but most of what I do relates back to this company Creative Productions, which was a very successful trade show builder in Pittsburgh. While I was there, I was able to meet a number of corporate people. Even to this day, there are clients that I have that descended from one or two original relationships through

Creative Productions, so I think it's important to remind young people to be careful when you're working. Make sure you're making the right relationships because they form the basis for a career.

Bill Flanagan: Executive Vice President, Corporate Relations, Allegheny Conference

This has been a learn on the job kind of experience in many ways because as a reporter I go out, I talk to people, I try to understand what the story was, and I tell people about it. In the case of working for the Allegheny Conference, I've had to dig a lot deeper into how things work, how you actually get things done, how you build consensus, and how you sell people on an idea in its early stages or convince them to go along with it.

A lot of what we do is partnering. We don't control a lot of the activities of other organizations that control communications channels about the region, so somehow we have to herd the cats, jolly everybody along, try to get everybody sort of centered and on the same page. It's sort of moving more or less in the same direction and that's something you learn by doing. They don't teach you how to do that in school. You kind of have to do it and get to know how people work, and then hopefully you can work together to get a good result.

Julie Smith: Principal/President RJW Media

The biggest influence I would have to say is my 15 years at DDF&M (Dudreck Depaul Ficco & Morgan Advertising). That's where I really learned everything. Running their media department for 15 years is where

I cut my teeth, and that's where I really learned how to develop the culture of customer service, which I carried over into my job today.

Don Decker: Regional Sales, Comcast Spotlight

Integrity in how I approach my job and interaction with clients and people in general. That carries through to the kind of results that I'm able to obtain and the relationships I've been able to make.

Rob Deaner: Founder/Composer, Market Street Sound

Every time I'm asked to do a record or create a piece of music or create an advertisement, do a voiceover, somebody's voice tape, even the simplest things, somebody is including me in achieving their dream. And that's a really cool thing to be able to do.

Guido D'Elia: Partner, Mind Over Media

I would say fear. I mean, I've never felt like I had the background for this business or for production or creative endeavors. I've never formally trained in any aspect of it, so I always feel like I need to work harder than the next guy, out think them, and that's been my motivator. I never get comfortable. I'm working on it though.

Discussion Questions

1. Is the Sender and Receiver Model for communication too simple, especially in a digital world? Should it be revised? Why or why not?

2. What is your communication process? How is it similar to or different from the processes described by the panelists?

3. What common themes in process did you notice between the panelists? Why do you think they share these views?

4. When discussing his process, Flanagan said, "You really have to understand who you're trying to talk to and what you want them to do." Why does he emphasize using communication to motivate action? Is this unique to business-oriented communication? Why or why not?

5. A few panelists emphasized the importance of face-to-face or direct communication. Do you agree or disagree? Why? Will face-to-face communication become less important in the future?

6. Do you have a mentor? How have they impacted your life? If you do not have a mentor, how can you go about finding one?

7. When Landesberg's father said, "My typewriter has the same number of keys as everybody else's, and my phone calls every other phone," what do you think he meant? Why is it important?

8. When Popović said he is "suspect of someone who doesn't have a process" what do you think he meant? Could the lack of process indicate the level or accomplishment of the professional?

Join the Conversation

Scan the QR codes from this section to watch the video for each question, then read the comments shared by others in our community. Add your thoughts to join our conversation.

Q4 | How do you define communications?

Q5 | What is your process for communicating?

Q6 | What is the biggest influence in how you communicate?

We drive into the future using only our rearview mirror.

- Marshall McLuhan, Canadian Philosopher of Communication Theory

Kevin Popović and Rob Deaner, producer of the *20YEARS* music soundtrack.
Photo courtesy of Jack Wolf.

Chapter 03 | Lessons Learned

Introduction

Not surprisingly, effective communication within the communications process is a recurring theme for this panel. As our panelists reflect on what they have learned in their careers and the mistakes that people within their disciplines and within business sometimes make, ineffective communication comes up again and again. A client failing to communicate effectively with his agency can cripple an account before it even begins. An agency failing to communicate effectively within its team and with its clients can be just as damning. And finally, the client and the agency both failing to communicate effectively with the target audience dooms the message to drift aimlessly in the deafening static of what has become "over communication." Effective communication is essential, yet it seems even seasoned veterans encounter communication challenges.

Recent research reveals that the general consumer made five percent fewer calls in 2012 than she did in 2011 while sending an average of 50 texts a week (Ofcon, 2012), and we have already noted the impact of electronic communications on our industry, but is it improving clarity?

As much as the growth of the Internet has benefited the communications industry by providing multiple new mediums for us to explore and leverage, the growing preference for email and texting may be hindering our work, which could affect our relationships with clients and with our coworkers. Even if the simplicity of texting makes it more attractive than placing a call or talking in person, that does not negate the existing body of research that supports face-to-face communication as the most effective way to share information (Doherty-Sneddon et al, 1997;Flaherty et al, 1998). Not only does face-to-face communication improve the chances of a message being delivered accurately, it also nurtures relationships, which as we learned in the previous chapter are important in the communications industry. Distance still matters, and face-to-face communication is still the most effective (Olson & Olson, 2000).

The Team

A few of the panelists emphasized how crucial a team can be, which includes but extends beyond opening and maintaining effective communication channels between the sometimes isolated members of an agency, company, or project. How you communicate with your team is important, but who you have on your team to communicate with is important as well. Jim Collins, a business consultant and the bestselling author of *Good to Great* (2006), describes this as getting the right people on the bus, or putting the "who before the what." If the right people are not on the bus, and the wrong people are not off the bus—Collins argues and supports with extensive primary and secondary research—an organization can struggle to collaborate and fail to overcome inevitable challenges. Having a strong team is key, and additional research supports Collins' already well-supported conclusions.

Development Dimensions International (DDI), a human resource consulting firm, and the Electronic Recruiting Exchange (ERE) collaborated on a survey of ERE's 550 online community members, which included members of the Fortune 100 and Global 2000 (Bernthal, 2001). They identified four common practices for ensuring that the right people were invited to join a company. Three of the four tactics focused specifically on skill and ability: screening resumes with an automated system, asking candidates to relate examples of when they had to use certain skills, and simulating workplace challenges. The fourth tactic focused exclusively on whether or not candidates' motivations and personalities aligned with the values of the hiring company and its workflow process, which is to say how well each candidate would fit in a particular environment. These are great companies focused on hiring great people, just as Collins' advocates and just as some of our panelists, experienced and successful professionals themselves, felt was important enough to point out.

Being a Part of a Team

Being a contributing member of a team is a mix of communication skills and relevant ability. Designers should be good at designing. Writers should be good at writing. Composers should be good at composing. But we are no longer strictly divided by discipline. The struggling economy has eaten away at profits and starved budgets, forcing an already highly competitive market to be even more competitive. For communications professionals, this means that companies are looking for recruits who are versatile and who can satisfy multiple needs at once. Hart Research Associates (2010), working with the Association of American Colleges and Universities, interviewed 302 employers and found that employers are looking for recruits with broad skill sets, not just singular specialties. They also demand a highly developed ability to learn and acquire new knowledge. For us, communications is and has been a rapidly evolving field. The ability to adapt to new technologies and market shifts is necessary for survival, and that adaption now has to include a diverse collection of abilities as well. Our panelists agree with the research, but at least one panelist is not happy about the direction this trend is steering communications.

The proliferation of technology has made the once niche tools of communication professionals available to the masses. Hobbyists are learning Photoshop and Illustrator, high school students are publishing Flash animations, and nearly every member of the first world owns a digital camera in the form of a cell phone, an affordable point and click model, or both. Newgrounds. Flickr. YouTube. The masses are making and sharing media. Thomas Werner (2011), a Former Director for the American Society of Media Photographers (AMSP), says, “Photography isn’t dead, but the old business model is.” He goes on to say that the industry has changed dramatically, which will ultimately create more opportunities in the future. Not all experts will agree with Werner, and it would seem that even some of our panelists disagree, but our panelists are in total agreement on one matter: things will change, and if you want to stay in this business you have to be able to change along with it.

The Audience

Once we have communicated effectively with the client and our team, our next challenge is to communicate effectively with our target audience. According to our panelists, one of the most common mistakes on this front is failing to perform or trust in the research. The literature overwhelmingly agrees that research is a necessity (Broom & Dozier, 1990; Austin & Pinkleton, 2009). It provides insight into a target audience. It provides context. It reveals opportunities and challenges. Perhaps most importantly, research helps to eliminate the assumptions or bias of a creative team. We cannot possibly expect ourselves or our team to intuitively understand every possible audience, and failing to realize this can hurt the message, our business, and our clients' business. Ignoring the importance of research is a mistake that will undermine the communications process. Admittedly, there are many more challenges in communicating with an audience, and we explore those challenges in greater depth in the next two chapters.

20 Years of Lessons

Our panelists hail from different backgrounds, professionally and personally, but they have all learned a great deal from their 20 years in communications. Their observations are framed and informed by their unique experiences, and the common themes that emerge from our open-ended questions suggest that these themes are worth exploring more deeply. If we can learn from these giants, we can stand on their shoulders and continue to advance communications.

Q7 | What have you learned about your part of the communications process?

Brian Bronaugh: President/Executive Creative Director, Mullen – Pittsburgh
The philosophical answer is that I'm still learning. I don't think I've got the complete answer to that question.

I have found out that communications is extremely hard work to do. Trying to convince people inside your shop, your clients, and then the targets we're trying to communicate with to believe in something, to take an action, is extremely hard work. If you don't have a passion for it, if you don't believe in what it is you're doing, what will it come to?

Rob Deaner: Founder/Composer, Market Street Sound
In terms of music, music is really hard. It is an old man's game. It is something that is really difficult to do effectively consistently. There are a lot of people who do it, and there are a lot of people who make money doing it.

I take it very seriously because it is something I've done all my life. What I've learned is that I know very little about it, and every opportunity I have to do something I learn. I'm constantly teaching myself.

And what I've learned through the years… when you are a young man and full of confidence and a few people have told you that you are reasonably good at what you do, you start to believe that. You need confidence to be a musician, to be a composer, because you have to believe your ideas have merit. You know that they are worth working on it, worth developing, and worth sharing. But when you are young you tend to think, at least I did, that maybe I know more than I do, or that I can conquer any mountain without fear. I've learned that being a better communicator is to be quiet and to be still, to learn what the situation needs rather than dictating to the situation.

Glenn Przyborski: Director/Cinematographer, Przyborski Productions

We always used to think that ad agency guys all sat around and just worried about TV, and then when you're around a lot of them you realize TV is probably ten percent of what they do, so I'm a little more aware of what's going on with people that work in that business.

We've also found that our approach is a little better when we're dealing with clients that are a little bit older and I say that because we can show 12 different ways of doing something. A lot of people are like, 'Oh my God! He's just figured out a way of having some crazy effect or whatever.'

You'll find an older person, especially in today's economy, that works at an ad agency or that works as a client, they'll sort of want to hire someone that's been around the block a few times rather than the latest, greatest happened upon the scene.

Rick Landesberg: Principal, Landesberg Design

I have learned that there's a difference between my personal agenda and the agenda of my office or the agenda of my colleagues and clients. It's important to keep those separate. In other words, there are things that I care about. Tastes, inclinations, interests, and curiosities—that's my business, and I care about that. That's important, but it's separate from what the client cares about. And it's very important to know their agenda. What's on their minds?

I once got some great advice that had to do with presenting to clients: tell them why they should like it. It doesn't matter if I like it. In fact, it's presumed I like it, and it doesn't matter. When you're in a restaurant, and some kid who's a waiter says, "I like the salmon." Well, what do I care if you like the salmon? If everyone's buying the salmon, and they're selling out the salmon every night—it's that good—that's different. So when I present to a client, I've learned to talk about what they care about. In fact, what's even more important is what does the client's client care about? What does that ultimate user, the ultimate audience, care about?

Julie Smith: Principal/President RJW Media

There has been a change. The Internet of course, while it still has a ways to go, has made a huge impact on our industry.

When RJW Media first opened its doors in 1985, the choices weren't as abundant in the media world. There were two newspapers, the Pittsburgh Press and the Post Gazette. There were four network TV stations, a couple of independents and a handful of cable networks. Cable at that time was thought of more as a utility. People subscribed to cable to get better reception for the networks. Today it's completely different. And the choices. Who goes to newspapers to look up information? They go to the Internet. Who goes to the Yellow Pages to look up a phone number? If you want directions, use your mobile phone.

Raelin Sawka Musuraca: Digital Strategist

When it comes to communicating, it's not just about the medium. Digital strategy isn't really about what kind of website you can have or what kind of online banner you can have; it's still about communicating. Often times people get afraid of the medium. They get too worried about how a website works or how this social media stuff works, and they forget about communicating. I've always got to bring them back around to what it is that we want to communicate, not how we want to communicate or what tool we want to use to communicate with.

Bill Flanagan: Executive Vice President, Corporate Relations, Allegheny Conference

Good communication comes from an understanding of your target audience, who you're trying to communicate with.

At the end of the day you really have to understand who you're trying to talk to and what you want them to do and that's usually the first question I'll ask of anybody. We'll always sit down and we'll ask them first – what are you trying to get done and who are you trying to influence to get it done? And that becomes really the beginning of everything we do and I think I've learned that along the way.

Mike Lee: Founder/Executive Producer, Studious One

What I've learned about communications, and this applies to everybody that is in the field of communications, is that one of the most difficult things is to communicate well with each other on a project. The irony of that right? Public relations and creative and producers like me—oftentimes the communications within us is lacking. It's a skill in and of itself to be able to work with other people.

Kevin Popović: Founder of Ideahaus

My part of the process has evolved over the last 20 years.

Early in my process, my part was to help educate clients as to what communications can do for them. Why they should do it. And that process has changed over the years, both in the type of work that we do and in my own personal perspective. I've resolved myself that I'm done being John the Baptist. No more conversions. You either believe in communications and what it's going to do for you, or you don't. That's fine if you don't, but have fun in hell.

My job today is to help clients who are prepared to invest in communications, who want to communicate with their customers, to help them figure out what to say and how to say it first, and then to look at the channel or the technology second.

Saul Markowitz: President, Markowitz Communications

A lot of other presidents of agencies like to outsource work or hand it off to someone else on the staff. "This is your story; go do it." What I've learned on the process side of it is that I really enjoy being in the process. Even if I'm behind the scenes I still need to be a part of it. I have a feeling when I'm 90 or 100 years old I'm still going to be the one driving out looking for the – if there's a print story, which unfortunately there might not be a lot of print but still, you know – I'm the one that gets up at 5 in the morning looking for the newspaper box trying to find that story again to see if it was done right. It's really great going online at midnight because you know it's about to hit, and I'm sitting there, and I can't go to sleep until I see if what we did ended up correctly. And so, really my process is being in the middle of it and being a real big part of it.

Chauncey Smith: Chief Sales and Marketing Director, ScienceMedia

It has to seamlessly work across the various components. It can't function in its own silo. It can't stand out in and amongst itself. It has to work synergistically with the other parts of the communication plan to really get the maximum effect.

David Sladack: VP & Group Account Strategy Director, Brunner Advertising

When I was younger, my role was more defined. It may have focused on one area of this communications process or it focused just on the communications, but a couple things happen. One, you gain a lot of experience, and you become someone who's trusted by your client to do more than just the communications. You take on a much larger role. Very, very often when I work with clients, I work on everything but the communications. I'll work on brand strategy. I'll work on product development. I'll work on pricing and etcetera. My position really does encompass a lot more than just communications in today's advertising world.

Roy Cheran: Director of Business Development, Mind Over Media

For most of my career in the business I've sat on the partner side, those that initiate the strategy and communications. The most critical piece of that is that customers and partners are looking to you and your organization as being experts in the field. You need to take a leadership position in the dialogue and in developing the strategy and making recommendations. It's necessary to do that to be an effective and valued partner.

Don Decker: Regional Sales, Comcast Spotlight

It's the timing of the communications and getting back and responding to people I'm trying to do business with or production houses, communicating to them quickly what we need as far as material and keeping things moving forward as smoothly as possible. I find the best thing is open communication. It's got to be back and forth, responsive.

Michael Hills: Vice President/General Manager, Comcast Spotlight

This is going to be a little cliché. My part is assembling the absolute best team of people to help our advertisers do the job of communicating. Everybody talks about hiring being the most important thing you can do, but I don't think people really believe it. When you actually believe and act on that and you hire the best possible people for any position that you're hiring for, you can create a team of people that can move the world. And advertising is a tool that you can move the world with, so to me the most important thing I can do is hire great talent.

Michael Lotenero: Designer/Artist, Michael Lotenero Art + Design

In terms of illustration and design, it's changed so much. The old days of the creative director sketching on a napkin and passing it down to the art directors and designers—they don't really exist that way anymore. Everyone needs to think on their feet and be fairly good at everything. Not just fairly good, but really good. I know people that specialize, and that's great, but it's also nice when you're working with a writer that makes music or a creative director that does design. Everybody is essentially a creative director or art director. Everyone is really talented now. Everybody is doing great work, so it's competitive.

Jack Wolf: Commercial Photographer, Wolf Photography

That it's diminished. Every kid has a camera. "Oh, we don't need stills, somebody will shoot it off their phone," so my part's diminished because it doesn't seem to be that important anymore. It's that "caveman" thing.

Anybody can do it, so it's been reduced, minimalized. It's very depressing.

Paige Beal: Assistant Professor, Marketing & Advertising, Point Park University

I've learned to be flexible and to embrace change and to understand that I'm a lifelong learner. You have to constantly be looking for how you integrate the next piece of technology into the whole mix, and it's a challenge. It's a significant challenge for everybody, but that's been the biggest challenge and lesson.

Guido D'Elia: Partner, Mind Over Media

As an entrepreneur trying to build a business we always tried to build an environment where people could come and do their work and felt good about doing what they were doing. We tried to get people in the environment that work well with each other, and where everyone kind of feels comfortable doing what is right – a very tricky thing and subjective solution. People with like minds that want to do good work to create and have a business that flourishes. So that's been our model from the beginning, create the right environment.

Dennis Moran: Principal, Dennis Moran Design

This is something I'm looking at being around for several decades. I like to think that the things that I'm developing or designing are holistic. They are things that would cut across the entire breadth of an organization. Although it's a very small part of a much bigger communication issue, it's one that slices right through the center. It's one that literally would have impact across all of them.

If I do my job right, I'm creating an antibiotic, if you will, that is full spectrum. It's a full spectrum antibiotic that would be delivered in a lot of different ways. It's an injectable. It's a tablet, a pill. Hopefully it'll last a long time as well.

Q8 | What is the biggest mistake practitioners make in communications?

Roy Cheran: Director of Business Development, Mind Over Media

The biggest mistake we make as practitioners is thinking too much of ourselves. There are still a vast number of people in our business that think it's all about them versus all, and oh, by the way, if your skills and talents and abilities allow you to assist the customer, that's great.

The focal point should be on what the customer's needs are versus serving my own self-fulfilling prophecy. You will get there if you help people.

Jack Wolf: Commercial Photographer, Wolf Photography

We don't have enough respect for our clients. I think the clients are put upon because you go to the meeting and you schmooze the guy or the woman and everything is cool. Then you go back and talk about them. Did you hear what he said? She's going to be really bad. How we going to get around this?

You better pay attention: you better love your clients because they've got the bucks. They're the only people with any money. Where would you be if you didn't get paid for what you did?

Dennis Moran: Principal, Dennis Moran Design

It relates to people. Our gravest errors are in not understanding the human aspect of it. We either haven't done a good enough job to find out how we should be talking to those people, understanding them, reaching them. We sometimes make the message too complicated. We're not considering it from their viewpoint.

The things that work best are those that are simple and direct, and they consider the human condition of the audience very carefully.

Michael Hills: Vice President/General Manager, Comcast Spotlight

The biggest mistake is that people tend to use electronic media, and there are lots of forms of it, as a replacement for human communication. The Internet has changed the world. Social media will change the world. Mobile media has changed the world. Email has obviously changed the world.

Look at the post office scenario. The post office can't do what they do anymore because it's been replaced largely by email. Those are all amazing tools, but you cannot use them to replace face to face communication.

Rob Deaner: Founder/Composer, Market Street Sound
So now I think what I've learned in being a better communicator is to be quiet and to be still, and to, and to learn maybe what the situation needs rather than me dictating to the situation.

Rick Landesberg: Principal, Landesberg Design
Whether we're designers or communicators of any kind, we have to understand the difference between our problem, our task, and the client's concern.

Kevin Popović: Founder of Ideahaus

As a group, I see the biggest mistake being that the different parts of the communications process works in these silos. The separatist attitude between some of the disciplines has made it more difficult for others included in the process, and it's made it not as beneficial for our clients. Whether you're in a marketing firm or an advertising firm or you're a PR agency or a design shop or web development or whomever—you are a part of this process. Play well with others. Try to be a little less territorial. Try to be a little more open for the client's benefit.

Bill Flanagan: Executive Vice President, Corporate Relations, Allegheny Conference
Traditional agencies and traditional communicators can become very

frustrated in a community environment because they keep wondering who's going to make the decision. Why do you keep changing things? Why isn't there more money? Those kind of issues. I found, in the last year working for the conference, that there's tension among a number of the firms we've had to work with because they just don't understand what it's like to work in an environment where it's all done by consensus. It's all collaboration, and often you cannot control what your partners do. You jolly them along. You try to encourage them. If you give them clear enough, concise enough, creative enough communication tools, it's amazing what you can get people to do in a spirit of partnership, but getting to that point can be a very painful process.

Julie Smith: Principal/President RJW Media

A mistake is thinking you can accomplish your goals with just one medium. In today's world, there's a mix. Twenty years ago, you could have satisfied your whole campaign and reached all of your customers with a television campaign. Today, TV's a part of that, but you need much more to reach the same number of people because they're consuming media in many different ways. You can't reach the masses anymore in just one place.

Don Decker: Regional Sales, Comcast Spotlight

Over-complicating the message. Looking at it too deeply. Sometimes less can be more, a simpler approach, depending on how the message is positioned to customers or clients. An over complication of that leads to confusion or problems.

Michael Lotenero: Designer/Artist, Michael Lotenero Art + Design
Before you waste a lot of time and energy, figure out the best way to get their point across.

Raelin Sawka Musuraca: Digital Strategist
There are two. The first one is that we get caught up in with what we think is cool from a digital perspective. Coming in and saying, "I saw this. This is neat, and let's do it." And not really thinking about what the audience needs. A lot of people come to me and want to do a cool Flash piece when really all they need is a sales flyer. They need a printed piece of material.

The other mistake is that a lot of times businesses will short change the research just because of budget. You have to do the research to get in the target audience's shoes and really understand them. If you don't have the time or the budget to do all the research, there are lots of ways to do the research, to get that mindset, to really understand that target audience within the budget that you have. To not take that time to do the research, to short change it, is really just being lazy.

David Sladack: VP & Group Account Strategy Director, Brunner Advertising
First, we occasionally do not have the right insights, and when you don't have the right insights through research, primary or secondary, you don't have the understanding. Then you don't really gather that meaningful selling proposition. The second piece is that sometimes the mechanism or the execution can overpower the message. What I mean by that is sometimes the creative, or the method that we use to get the message across, can get in the way of the message and confuse the customer.

Paige Beal: Assistant Professor, Marketing & Advertising, Point Park University
There's that constant pressure with the client to hear what they have to say and you have to listen, but the client isn't necessarily the end all. It's that constant being on the edge, keeping the client happy but yet doing what needs to be done. Oftentimes, a client is not looking at the big picture because they're so meshed. They have the blinkers on, and they're working really hard to try to take themselves out of that and look objectively at their own business, but it's difficult if not impossible to do it.

It can be a constant battle. "You say you're trying to do this, but I'm looking at this body of research, which really tells me you ought to be going in this direction." It's a challenge.

Chauncey Smith: Chief Sales and Marketing Director, ScienceMedia

To me, effective communication is both art and science. And there is a lot of emphasis, on the part of agencies, put on the creative and the emotional side of communication, and that's relevant. Where it could be tightened is how it supports the business's agenda and whatever that business's milestone is, whether it's awareness or conversion rate. We should be able to speak directly as to how the communication plan that's being presented is going to impact those key attributes.

Brian Bronaugh: President/Executive Creative Director, Mullen – Pittsburgh

We don't make enough mistakes. We don't take risks. We don't push. We don't fail forward. We don't find out what is working. More importantly, we don't find out what's not working quickly.

There's an aversion, there's a fear that we operate under a lot, and I think any business operates under that to some degree or another, but I would say that the fear of failure is a mistake.

Mike Lee: Founder/Executive Producer, Studious One

The chances that we take are leveled off because we have to be concerned with money, with our client's approval, with whatever purpose they're doing this project for. The greatest work, I think, comes in times where you can almost expect failure. You're taking a chance. You're really putting it out there. Not taking chances lends itself to a lot of mediocrity, unfortunately.

Saul Markowitz: President, Markowitz Communications
Doing the same old, same old. Seriously.

Glenn Przyborski: Director/Cinematographer, Przyborski Productions
The biggest mistake I see happening is when someone gets locked into a concept. Maybe it's something crazy like a guy screaming at the camera, and suddenly they'll try to transpose an idea that they liked or that they caught off of television into a client that has absolutely no relationship with that. I have seen so many corny ideas that we've been involved in, and they exist solely because someone liked the idea and just assumed it would transpose to an audience.

If you're dealing with an audience that's 65 years old and is worried about healthcare, about some heart problem or something, a teenage-appropriate idea frequently doesn't work, yet we see that all the time.

Guido D'Elia: Partner, Mind Over Media
The easiest mistake to trap yourself into is to look for the solution you want to do, and apply it to whatever it is that's brought to you as a challenge just because you want to do it. To talk yourself into that is the biggest problem with this business in general. Your personal preference is something you've been influenced by, and it can jump in place of what is really needed and should be the right thing to do.

Q9 | What is the biggest mistake businesses make in communications?

Michael Hills: Vice President/General Manager, Comcast Spotlight
From an advertising standpoint in that part of communications, I think the biggest mistake being made now is that people don't react fast enough to the changes in media. People aren't following the eyeballs fast enough.

There's so much change that's happened in the past five years—let alone the past 20 years—in terms of the Internet, social media, and mobile media and all the things that are replacing traditional media to some extent, like satellite radio, iPods, podcasting. There are so many tools out there that I think businesses hang on too long to what they used to do because they were comfortable with it, and they're losing opportunities because they don't advertise effectively. You have to follow where the eyeballs are going, and the eyeballs are moving. They're going to a lot of different directions.

Don Decker: Regional Sales, Comcast Spotlight

Too many layers. Too many directions that they want to take a message. Not staying on point. Trying to be all things to all people when a less complicated, simpler message could be best to help define them, their brand, and their business.

Paige Beal: Assistant Professor, Marketing & Advertising, Point Park University

We're getting much larger generational divides in behavior, so I see that as still being the biggest difficulty.

Not understanding the target market or presuming that they know more about the target market than they do. They assume that they don't have to do the research in order to understand them. I see that so consistently that it's really frightening. And I think the target markets have to get narrower, and I'm still hearing stuff like 25 to 54, 18 to 49, and honest to

God what does one have to do with another? Nothing.

Glenn Przyborski: Director/Cinematographer, Przyborski Productions
A lot of clients hire ad agencies because of their name, because they've been in the business the longest, but what they don't realize is that typically four people are on your account. You got a great account executive, an art director, a writer, and maybe a creative person that oversees the whole thing. Even though that agency may have 100 people, those are the only four that are going to be doing your account. A lot of people don't realize that when you deal with the bigger ad agencies.

They don't think they're going to get the junior guys because typically some high-powered creative director does the sales pitch, and they do the whole nine yards of the presentation. Ultimately, since he's not there and sets the account next to the bottom as far as account size, the junior kids are going to be working on that account. It may not be bad if the junior kids are talented, but frequently clients think they've hired an agency because of the main guys, but they have nothing to do with their account other than reviewing it every few months.

Bill Flanagan: Executive Vice President, Corporate Relations, Allegheny Conference
For a lot of businesses, the internal fight often seems to be within the legal department and the marketing department and the advertising department. Trying to square that away so that you can be forthright is important. Personally, I think it's always best to say something, to always be truthful, rather than to say nothing or to do a no comment.

At the end of the day, just as a reporter, if I felt that the company had always been truthful about how its product performs, about how the business does business, I would then give them the benefit of the doubt when they got into trouble or when something went wrong because I would say, "These folks are straight shooters, and I trust them. I'm going to make sure I tell their side of the story fairly when the going gets tough." There's a tendency inside a lot of businesses to sort of batten down the hatches, to control all the communication, to put the lawyers out front, and I think it works against them.

People tend to respond to organizations or individuals who are honest and truthful and are making an effort to do their job well.

Michael Lotenero: Designer/Artist, Michael Lotenero Art + Design

Businesses should just be honest about what they really do. We all watch Mad Men with the cigarette ads and all the glamour days of people being very easily lied to, but audiences are pretty savvy now. It's really important to take the viewer into consideration. I have a 13-year old son, and you can't get anything past him. It's like they see right through it. They know when something's hokey. They know when something's not authentic, when it's not really cool or is just pretending to be cool.

People are afraid to have the balls to actually do something that is awesome and honest because they're afraid that people aren't going to get it. The most successful stuff is the stuff that pushes it.

David Sladack: VP & Group Account Strategy Director, Brunner Advertising

The number one biggest mistake that business make: they're a little heavy handed in the sales process. They want the sales message to come across a little too heavy, and in today's world you can't do that. It has to be a more authentic process. And secondly, perhaps, I've seen businesses not give the customer enough credit of having an intuitive process of their own to figure things out.

Guido D'Elia: Partner, Mind Over Media

Is it more important to address their audience or five or six people down the hall? That's been since the beginning of time. Everyone has a job, and everyone would like to keep their job. Everyone has bosses. That influence can be a little too strong, though. That influence should always be there because that person is supposed to influence the person who is doing that communications piece, but if it's too strong and if they are too worried about that, then you miss an opportunity to connect.

Rick Landesberg: Principal, Landesberg Design

There's nothing better than being offered the opportunity to do good work for good people who are doing smart things. On occasion, you see clients not do well or even fail, and sometimes they fail because they forget who they're working for. Sometimes you work for a client whose attention is more on who's down the hall. It's like the comedian who's telling jokes to the band instead of to the audience. But when they're focused on who they're really working for, good things happen.

Raelin Sawka Musuraca: Digital Strategist

I think the biggest mistake they make is they go by what they like or their wife likes, and I really hope a lot of clients don't see this, but it's the truth. It's what my son or daughter likes or they react to, and they don't think about the target audience. They think they know based on their own reaction, and they really have to let the professionals do the job and present to them.

We make a mistake by not sharing that information with them, by not preparing them, by not saying we did it this way because your target audience reacts to blue or your target audience reacts well to these key phrases, but we have to keep it about that audience, and I think a lot of times they forget about that.

Chauncey Smith: Chief Sales and Marketing Director, ScienceMedia

We call on an awful lot of the big pharmaceutical companies. They are just a little afraid to experiment with some of the new channels. There are opportunities within social media for big pharmaceutical companies to really leverage and build some customer intimacy and record of knowledge on them, but there's this perceived threat of information getting out that shouldn't in an un-sanitized or un-reviewed sort of way. That is a risk, but that risk shouldn't outweigh some of the benefits that social media and some of the evolving channels for communication offer.

Mike Lee: Founder/Executive Producer, Studious One

The clients themselves sometimes aren't willing to take the chance. Although I will say this, there are some clients that are the crazy ones, and you have to bring them back down to Earth. In either case I think, the biggest mistake they make is not listening to the people that they hire, who are the experts. Clients are paying the bills at the end of the day, and that's going to win out, but if you really want to do something great, you should be willing to listen.

Kevin Popović: Founder of Ideahaus

The biggest mistake I see businesses make on a recurring basis is to think that there's a magic bullet, whether it's a business that thinks they can continue to have a leading presence and communicate in some sort of quality with half their budget, or doing part of it in house, or just getting by, or "We'll only do this," but still having very large expectations of those of us involved with it.

Julie Smith: Principal/President RJW Media

Cutting their marketing and advertising budget and really not being open to trying any of the new options that are out there. That's it in a nutshell.

Jack Wolf: Commercial Photographer, Wolf Photography

A lot of them don't have any respect for the creative process. They just think you hire somebody to do a camera. "Oh, you mean you need to light it? What do you mean you need to light it? It's going to take how long? Oh man, I didn't know that."

They have no understanding. They think point and shoot, and we'll get it done in no time. "Is this really going to take this long? Why do we need makeup? We don't need makeup." They don't get our part of it because they've never been on a set. They don't really understand what it takes.

Brian Bronaugh: President/Executive Creative Director, Mullen – Pittsburgh

What I've seen with the wide variety of clients that we've worked with is that really good clients utilize you as a partner. They give you a seat at the table. They're engaging you in the overall strategic vision of what it is they want to accomplish. The ones that utilize you as a vendor, they're just checking off a box. I don't think that's really the best way to utilize the kind of minds that we employ.

Roy Cheran: Director of Business Development, Mind Over Media

They don't know this, but they are very challenged to understand who they are and, more importantly, who they need to be to those target audiences. There is inbred bias, daily opinion polls at the water cooler. They just have too much head trash about who they are, what they do, and how they go about their business. They can benefit significantly from dialogue with an outside party who is at a 70,000 foot level, breathing clear air with a clean vision of what they need to do to get where they want to go.

My best advice would be: don't be as guarded, don't think you are holding the keys to the candy store, don't be afraid to share your story with people outside the organization who can really help you develop a better strategy, craft a better message, and develop a much more effective implementation plan for a particular communications strategy.

Rob Deaner: Founder/Composer, Market Street Sound

People believe that they've got more answers than they do. What I see is people hiring people to do jobs and not letting them do them. I see clients hiring agencies and not letting the agency help them. I see agencies hiring vendors and not letting the vendor do what it is they are good at. I see the communication process being stopped. It's a lot of one-way communication.

People are afraid to make decisions and afraid to take responsibility because you know there's a real monetary threat. An agency doesn't want to lose a client, so they don't want to educate their clients and tell them,

"You are not right, and you don't have the answer. You hired us to have the answer, take our advice." I don't see people standing up for that.

Saul Markowitz: President, Markowitz Communications

Sure, they know how to do public relations. Simple. And they know how to do creative. They get it because they have a cousin that used to do it. Right?

This is great thing that I learned from Don Hale. When I first started the business, I called him and said "I'm a little nervous now because I have my own staff now." He said, "Hire good people, and let them do their job." Unfortunately, sometimes clients will hire you, and they say you're the expert and then they forget. They totally forget the reason they hired you.

Discussion Questions

1. How important is research? What is your research process and how does it inform your communications planning?

2. What is the biggest mistake that you see communications professionals making? How can it be corrected?

3. What is the biggest mistake in communications that you have made? How did you learn from it?

4. When discussing what he has learned in 20 years, Popović said, "I've resolved myself that I'm done being John the Baptist. No more conversions. You either believe in communications and what it's going to do for you, or you don't." Speculate as to what drove him to this position. How would this mindset affect his business? What opportunities and challenges would it create?

5. What is your ideal team and work environment? Why?

6. What can be done to improve communication with your current team?

7. How can we overcome the proliferation of accessible technology that has Jack Wolf so depressed?

8. Brian Bronaugh commented that we are too afraid of making mistakes. Do you agree or disagree? Why? How can we create an environment that encourages taking risks without hurting business?

Join the Conversation

Scan the QR codes from this section to watch the video for each question, then read the comments shared by others in our community. Add your thoughts to join our conversation.

Q7 | What have you learned about your part of the communications process?

Q8 | What is the biggest mistake practitioners make in communications?

Q9 | What is the biggest mistake businesses make in communications?

The newest computer can merely compound, at speed, the oldest problem in the relations between human beings, and in the end the communicator will be confronted with the old problem, of what to say and how to say it.

- Edward R. Murrow, American Journalist

Kevin Popović with Guido D'Elia before his interview.
Photo courtesy of Jack Wolf.

Chapter 04 | Challenges in Delivering a Message

Introduction

In 2010, a Gallup poll found that 57 percent of Americans say that they "have little or no trust in the mass media to report the news fully, accurately, and fairly," adding a fourth year to a continuing trend (Morales). Additionally, 63 percent of Americans perceive news reporting as biased toward the right in some cases and the left in others.

According to a poll conducted by the Pew Research Center (2009), 63 percent of Americans believe that news stories are routinely inaccurate, a record high in 20 years. Sixty percent of respondents believe that news organizations are politically biased and that only 21 percent of news organizations are willing to admit their mistakes. The survey also found that this mistrust is largely nonpartisan, with respondents from across the political spectrum expressing their distrust.

Though we may not be journalists or news anchors, this general distrust is a challenge for communications. Our messages, whether they are in the form of print advertisements, online advertisements, television commercials, or occupying some other medium, are indirectly associated with the programming and writing that runs alongside of them. If an audience is skeptical of a message before we even have a chance to craft it, we are immediately starting at a disadvantage, at the bottom of an uphill battle. In the previous chapter, the importance of understanding a target audience through research was repeated again and again by the panelists, and this mistrust seems to be a lasting characteristic of nearly any target audience.

Spin, Spin, Spin

When asked about challenges in public relations, many of our panelists immediately identified obstacles like spin, truth, and transparency, and they had similar responses for advertising. Based on their answers, it would seem that perhaps the public mistrust for media is not unfounded.

In the book, *Toxic Sludge is Good For You: Lies, Damn Lies and the Public Relations Industry*, John Stauber and Sheldon Rampton (2002) analyze some of the largest public relations manipulations, using the 1975 Three Mile Island incident—where a spokesperson described how an ignited bubble of hydrogen could create a "spontaneous energetic disassembly"—as one of their major examples of public relations spin.

Many other books and articles have been written on the increase and power of public relations spin. In fact, there is no shortage of research on the topic. *A Century of Spin: How Public Relations Became the Cutting Edge of Corporate Power* describes how public relations, in the form of corporate propaganda, has shaped the modern world (Miller & Dinan, 2008). "*PR Must Die: Spin, Anti-Spin, and Political Public Relations in the UK, 1997-2004*" explores how spin has become an international phenomenon that has affected the political process as well (McNair, 2004). The research suggests, as our panelists did, that spin is a significant problem in communications.

And that problem is not isolated to public relations alone. Consumers are skeptical of advertising as well, though to varying degrees. Advertising has long attracted criticism, especially from authors like Jean Kilbourne (1999) who argue that advertising negatively manipulates consumers, warping their perception of reality and in some cases causing psychological harm. Her book *Deadly Persuasion: Why Women and Girls Must Fight the Addictive Power of Advertising* and her video series *Killing Us Softly: Advertising's Image of Women* (Sut, 1999) are common discussion topics in advertising courses nationwide.

Though Kilbourne's work is unrelentingly harsh on advertising, her distrust is not unique. *The 2012 Nielsen Global Trust in Advertising Survey* found that consumer trust in paid television, magazine, and newspaper ads dropped 24 percent, 20 percent, and 25 percent from 2009 levels, leaving roughly 47 percent of consumers trusting in paid advertising (Grimes, 2010). This near 50 percent level is consistent with other advertising research, where consumers were found to be relatively indifferent toward advertising, neither strongly trusting nor distrusting (Soh et al, 2007). Consumers may not be as skeptical of traditional advertising as they are of public relations, but the Nielson survey describes a trend that should interest any communications professional.

Randall Beard, global head, Advertiser Solutions at Nielsen, says, "Although television advertising will remain a primary way marketers connect with audiences due to its unmatched reach compared to other media, consumers around the world continue to see recommendations from friends and online consumer opinions as by far the most credible. As a result, successful brand advertisers will seek ways to better connect with consumers and leverage their goodwill in the form of consumer feedback and experiences" (Grimes, 2012).

Marketing and Social Media

The biggest challenges in marketing, as described by the experts that we interviewed, are creating true advocates and effectively delivering a message to a target audience. Supporters of social media would argue, however, that social media offers the solution for these challenges. As Beard commented earlier, recommendations from friends and online consumer opinions are trusted most by consumers, and social media would seem to be the best tool for fostering and leveraging that positivity in a target audience. In 2000, *The Cluetrain Manifesto*, one of the first books on the power the Internet would have on marketing, was published (Locke et al). It documented a change in the market that is now well-known to most communication professionals: consumers were having their own conversations about products, in the form of reviews and ratings and forum posts. Corporations and organizations eventually realized that consumers, more and more, based purchasing decisions on these conversations and not on advertisements, which has now become the norm according to Nielsen.

Seth Godin describes this new marketing process as "permission marketing" (1999) which now incorporates the leveraging of social media to create advocates and spread what he calls an "ideavirus" (2001), while Charlene Li and Josh Bernoff (2011) talk about capturing the power of the "groundswell," the organic formation of communities and conversations online. Regardless of the preferred terms, the growth of social media is undeniable. According to Pew (2012), 85 percent of adults are using the Internet, and of those adults, 66 percent use some form of social networking. And adults over 65, approximately 53 percent, are logging on as well, with one third of them using social media.

Is social media the solution to all of our communications challenges? Unlikely, but the research and our panelists agree that it is a growing medium, and our target audiences are likely congregating there.

20 More Years of Messages

As we look ahead to the next 20 years, our future actions should be informed by our past experiences and by the observations of our peers. We know that in public relations and advertising, our messages are often assumed to be dishonest. In marketing, we know that consumers rely increasingly on online reviews and recommendations from friends to guide their decision making. We also know that, based on the sheer number of individuals using social media, our audiences are using social media to talk. They might be talking about our messages positively, negatively, or not at all, but they are talking. The future is unknown, but the insight of our panelists can help to prepare you for what lies ahead.

Q10 | What is the biggest challenge in Public Relations?

Rick Landesberg: Principal, Landesberg Design
Truth.

Dennis Moran: Principal, Dennis Moran Design
Probably credibility.

Roy Cheran: Director of Business Development, Mind Over Media
Newsworthiness.

Mike Lee: Founder/Executive Producer, Studious One
It's always been the same: honesty.

Jack Wolf: Commercial Photographer, Wolf Photography
Schmooze better. They schmooze all the time, but they're lousy schmoozers. That's what they do, public relations. They spin and schmooze. They've got to get a balance between the schmoozers and the schmoozing so that you can know that it's at least believable in some way.

Bill Flanagan: Executive Vice President, Corporate Relations, Allegheny Conference

Not having people assume it's all public relations. When you show up to tell a story, they assume that you're just a flack. How do you get beyond that? How do you establish trust? How do you make sure your communication, your message, is judged to be real and legitimate and valued and carried forward?

Chauncey Smith: Chief Sales and Marketing Director, ScienceMedia

The biggest challenge in public relations is the idea of transparency, the balance you have to walk between transparency and effective brand building. Now, that's not to say that they are necessarily in conflict with one another, but certainly the general publics expectation of them, in the case of big pharmaceutical companies, being very transparent in their actions and motives is important.

Certainly public relations has always been a tool, and certainly the downside is you have to limit the spin to really be as transparent as you want to be with your audience.

Saul Markowitz: President, Markowitz Communications

I think there is too much spinning going on. And the word spin should never be in any public relation person's vocabulary. This gets me crazy. Spinning in the PR vocabulary is to spin the truth. It means to lie to everyone. The word spin needs to leave the PR vocabulary completely.

Guido D'Elia: Partner, Mind Over Media

The biggest challenge today is that people are used to the spin. There is just no way around it. They start with the thought "This is going to be spun." The public now, compared to 10, 15, 20 years ago, is so tuned to it that you are not fooling anybody when you spin it, so you've got to start on that basis or you can't have a shot at connecting.

Kevin Popović: Founder of Ideahaus
The consumer is a cynic. Every time that a public relations piece comes out, in most cases, it looks like public relations or spin, and people smell it coming.

In recent news situations, we've been to a lot of the behind the scenes and that strategy behind it, and the conversation now is starting with "How are they going to spin it?" How does somebody do their job being critiqued right out of the gate? It's hard for PR to come off as not PR when they're doing their job. That's their challenge.

Brian Bronaugh: President/Executive Creative Director, Mullen – Pittsburgh
There's a question of who leads social media, and I think that can be a different answer for each agency, but the public relations folks, the engagement people really, have a chance to lead that charge. I would say that's both their challenge and opportunity.

Don Decker: Regional Sales, Comcast Spotlight
Responding quickly and on point with the message you know.

Michael Hills: Vice President/General Manager, Comcast Spotlight
There's so much clutter in efforts to do public relations, to get the message out, that it's difficult to get it to stand out.

Paige Beal: Assistant Professor, Marketing & Advertising, Point Park University
Every day the landscape changes with social media, which is a huge part of public relations, so the challenge is keeping up with that landscape.

David Sladack: VP & Group Account Strategy Director, Brunner Advertising
I'd like to see more integration. Especially working in an ad agency, it often seems that the PR is not fully integrated. Our firm does a pretty good job of it actually, but when you look around and see examples of work across the category, sometimes you can see there's a bit of disjointedness.

Raelin Sawka Musuraca: Digital Strategist
Public relations has a tendency to get a little soft, and I work hand-in-hand every day with a great PR director, and social media is a very big area for them. It kind of steps over and combines with the digital platform, but I think it is metrics. It needs measured more particularly than the social media, and they have a harder time doing that in industry. I understand why, but clients don't understand why.

Q11 | What is the biggest challenge in Advertising?

Roy Cheran: Director of Business Development, Mind Over Media
Egos.

Dennis Moran: Principal, Dennis Moran Design
It's too complicated, too complicated for a human being to understand and comprehend.

Rick Landesberg: Principal, Landesberg Design
Truth.

Mike Lee: Founder/Executive Producer, Studious One
Advertising inflation. The claims that product A does this, then product B does this, then product A has to say this, and then it gets to be too much.

People don't believe any of it anymore.

Saul Markowitz: President, Markowitz Communications
Lack of creativity.

Guido D'Elia: Partner, Mind Over Media
Keeping your ideas clean and not being influenced by what you want to do versus what needs to be done.

Brian Bronaugh: President/Executive Creative Director, Mullen – Pittsburgh
It's this idea of how quickly things are changing and being comfortable with that idea of being uncomfortable.

Bill Flanagan: Executive Vice President, Corporate Relations, Allegheny Conference
Clutter. It's like that's all there is. It's the web. It's stuff there. It's stuff here. It's television. It's just so much communication, how do you break through?

Michael Hills: Vice President/General Manager, Comcast Spotlight
People aren't following the eyeballs fast enough.

Kevin Popovic: Founder of Ideahaus
The biggest challenge in advertising is staying relevant. If advertising can't play well with these other mediums that are part of an integrated approach, they'll drop by the wayside sooner than they think. Print's dead. Television as we know it is getting its ass handed to it by On Demand, TiVo, and Hulu. It's just not the same as it used to be.

Glenn Przyborski: Director/Cinematographer, Przyborski Productions
Advertising has to relate to that audience that might buy their product or might show up at their place of business.

Michael Lotenero: Designer/Artist, Michael Lotenero Art + Design
Making it really effective. You go through the magazines, and a car ad is a car ad, and a food ad is a food ad. Everybody wants a nice car. Everybody wants to eat good food. How do you make that engaging and enticing? That's a tough sell. .It really is hard to be concise and cut through the clutter, I mean, that's a tough job. I don't think it's getting any easier.

Rob Deaner: Founder/Composer, Market Street Sound
Creating a message that effectively talks to who you are trying to talk to. In other words, finding a way to communicate so that somebody listens. Rises

above the din. There is so much clutter. How do you communicate over that?

Paige Beal: Assistant Professor, Marketing & Advertising, Point Park University

Media. Proliferation. The knowledge base necessary in order to be able to use it.

Chauncey Smith: Chief Sales and Marketing Director, ScienceMedia

The biggest challenge in advertising is the fragmentation of and the move away from broadcast media to reach big swaths of your target market. Target markets are being more tightly defined each and every day.

Julie Smith: Principal/President RJW Media

Media fragmentation. Marketers need to communicate, and there are just so many ways anymore to do it. The pie is there, and there are many small pieces in that pie now. As media and buyers, to know and find opportunities is a challenge.

Jack Wolf: Commercial Photographer, Wolf Photography

Finding clients with money. Nobody's got any money. Nobody's got a budget. The secretary will do it. She'll get it done. That's the biggest challenge: finding a good client that realizes you have to spend money to make money.

Don Decker: Regional Sales, Comcast Spotlight

Trying to talk with clients and businesses in challenging economic times. Trying to keep them spending for their business and keeping their dollars invested to grow their business when they have been pulling back a little.

Raelin Sawka Musuraca: Digital Strategist
Metrics. Being able to measure it. Being able to understand why it works or why it doesn't work.

David Sladack: VP & Group Account Strategy Director, Brunner Advertising
Advertising revolves around measurement. The fact that we can measure is a good thing. The fact that we can measure is a bad thing. We can now measure so we know more thoroughly how effective our programs are, but often those measurements don't tell the entire picture. Sometimes clients are led to believe some things based upon a little bit of data they gather from one specific initiative.

Q12 | What is the biggest challenge in Marketing?

David Sladack: VP & Group Account Strategy Director, Brunner Advertising
The biggest challenge in marketing today is how do you truly create advocacy?

Roy Cheran: Director of Business Development, Mind Over Media
Implementation.

Paige Beal: Assistant Professor, Marketing & Advertising, Point Park University
Actually marketing. Actually looking from a strategic overview with the research necessary at a specific target market and keeping that focus for the entire strategy.

Mike Lee: Founder/Executive Producer, Studious One
Effective integration.

Dennis Moran: Principal, Dennis Moran Design
Identifying what to do. Not what to sell, but what should you even be doing? What is it?

Don Decker: Regional Sales, Comcast Spotlight
The right message. Delivering the right message to the right audience.

Guido D'Elia: Partner, Mind Over Media
Understanding your audience. Being able to relate with what they need

and getting material out there that connects up.

Rick Landesberg: Principal, Landesberg Design
Truth.

Raelin Sawka Musuraca: Digital Strategist
The politics that people play. People don't realize all of the politics behind what they have to do. I've learned that after being in that role for a couple of years, and the politics are tremendously hampering in achieving goals in creativity.

Brian Bronaugh: President/Executive Creative Director, Mullen – Pittsburgh
How quickly things are changing and being comfortable with that idea of being uncomfortable. I think that the advertising and marketing dynamics are extremely similar.

Michael Hills: Vice President/General Manager, Comcast Spotlight

Too many competing marketing activities at once. There is a day for everything. Every cause has a certain day or a yellow ribbon or wristband or whatever it is, and there's so many of them that I don't think people are breaking through the clutter.

Bill Flanagan: Executive Vice President, Corporate Relations, Allegheny Conference
Understanding your customer, understanding the competitive environment, and then really being able to respond to that in a savvy way. The world is changing rapidly all the time. It's very fluid, which makes it harder to find

that customer and make sure you're communicating to them well.

Rob Deaner: Founder/Composer, Market Street Sound

The biggest challenge that I see in marketing is how to see effectively who you are and then how you tell others about that. A lot of people misread who they are and talk about who they want to be, or who they see themselves as, and there is a disconnect between the message and the product.

Kevin Popović: Founder of Ideahaus

Biggest challenge in marketing has got to be understanding who you're talking to. Marketing is notorious for focus groups and research and strategy and stats and all that stuff, but it continues to amaze me how little businesses know going into speaking or trying to speak to their markets.

Julie Smith: Principal/President RJW Media

Budget cuts.

Glenn Przyborski: Director/Cinematographer, Przyborski Productions

The biggest challenge in marketing is to try to figure out a way to take a limited amount of money today and divide it correctly between all these different mediums—web, TV, whatever—and make some sense of a marketing plan as opposed to taking all of your money and putting it into a TV or all of it into radio or all of it into print.

Chauncey Smith: Chief Sales and Marketing Director, ScienceMedia
Certainly as budgets get a little tighter, having all these channels to reach is a challenge. Prioritizing which channels are going to give you the most return for your dollar invested is tough, and it may be very different than it was five or 10 years ago.

Saul Markowitz: President, Markowitz Communications
Lack of creativity.

Jack Wolf: Commercial Photographer, Wolf Photography
People have to understand that they need to market, but they don't want to spend, and they don't have an understanding. You have to get over that with them. You have to tell them to be prepared.

Q13 | What is the biggest challenge in Social Media?

David Sladack: VP & Group Account Strategy Director, Brunner Advertising
The biggest challenge in social media is return on investment. It's all about ROI, and how you can measure social media is still the unknown.

Don Decker: Regional Sales, Comcast Spotlight
How is it defined? What's the result back from it if a client gets involved in it? What are they getting out of it? You're going to spend some money to get into it and develop it, but when it comes to the end of the month or a quarter, how is it defined for them? What kind of results do they see?

Brian Bronaugh: President/Executive Creative Director, Mullen – Pittsburgh
We've talked about this in the sense of fatigue. I would say the biggest challenge for social media, any new platform that comes up, is the wow factor. It's great, it's the new thing, and then I think there's a sense of where'd that go? I use Google Wave as an example. It seemed like it was going to be the next big thing and now it's on hiatus. They just didn't work the bugs out. Any social media channel is going to have to deal with some of that fatigue factor from folks like us and even the people out in the world using it.

Rick Landesberg: Principal, Landesberg Design
To keep the noise down. To actually have it be fun, flexible, and enlightening but not stupid.

Mike Lee: Founder/Executive Producer, Studious One
Noise. Social media in its infancy was successful because it was one to one. It was people. Now it's companies. Now companies are invading the space, and everybody will tune out after a while. It's happened in every other medium. It's going to happen in social media too.

Kevin Popović: Founder of Ideahaus

I think the biggest challenge for social media is to find out how to implement it for business. I know there are businesses that have been using social media sites and services for sales and marketing - we do it every day for our clients. A lot of people are trying to figure out their process. We figured out our process in *Satellite Marketing*, but we're all still learning.

All of the things that we already know from communications have a place in social media, the trick is putting that square peg in the appropriate square hole and communicating to that market like they've never been able to do before.

Social media is this perfect storm that includes all of the wonderful things in communications that we do already. Advertising, slogans and headlines and taglines and calls to action, design elements in the profile pictures, branding and the logos that we bring to these sites and services. The public relations in being able to speak to segmented markets in controlled environments. Multimedia being able to deliver interactive and video on an ever-increasing bandwidth. It's just amazing.

Raelin Sawka Musuraca: Digital Strategist
Social media's interesting because people want to treat it like a discipline. They want to treat it as something. A lot of people want to think that social media is Facebook or social media is YouTube. Those are some platforms and some pieces of it, and if you focus on those too much you're not really going to engage in the conversations that are being had by your brand. That's what social media is, not the technology platforms that it's on.

Rob Deaner: Founder/Composer, Market Street Sound
How do you stay consistent and compelling at the same time? If you are using it from a marketing standpoint, how do you keep a presence in front of people that might be following you or interacting with you and not talk about what you had for breakfast? At some point, you run out of things to say.

Jack Wolf: Commercial Photographer, Wolf Photography
Youbook and Facetube. I get them so confused. I never look at them. Why do I want to look at someone's picture that they didn't take or they aren't in a provocative position? I don't care. You know they send updates like "I'm in line at Starbucks now. I'm buying coffee." So what? I don't want to see your picture of you buying coffee. So what?

Roy Cheran: Director of Business Development, Mind Over Media
Understanding how your target markets currently interface with it and how that will continue to grow and proliferate.

Chauncey Smith: Chief Sales and Marketing Director, ScienceMedia
The big challenge in social media is prioritization. I myself am a LinkedIn user. I don't use Facebook. LinkedIn serves my purposes very well. I fit into a lot of customer segments where they would like to try and reach me by social media, but the degree to which you embrace it makes it a little challenging for where you put your emphasis.

Michael Lotenero: Designer/Artist, Michael Lotenero Art + Design
It's pretty incredible. YouTube is the first place they go to find out about anything. It took me awhile to figure out. "Oh, I can figure out how to

bake a cake on YouTube?" At first, you don't think of it that way, that someone's going to post a video that actually has some content to it.

Glenn Przyborski: Director/Cinematographer, Przyborski Productions

The challenge is the age barrier. I'm totally used to having people send me e-mails, and I don't check Facebook. We have a Facebook account only because you're supposed to have it I guess, but I don't check that all the time. And when I see people write about Farmville and all that other stuff I totally lose interest in it. I would rather have someone email me directly.

Bill Flanagan: Executive Vice President, Corporate Relations, Allegheny Conference

Just trying to keep up with it. Social media is a real conundrum for a lot of folks. I don't know, frankly, how much money to invest in it or how much time to put into it because I know in traditional media what the results are. I still don't really understand what can be accomplished there, and it's all moving so fast that it's hard to keep up with.

Michael Hills: Vice President/General Manager, Comcast Spotlight

I think the biggest challenge in social media is that people haven't figured out how to use it for the sake of marketing or advertising or communications in general. Social media is a very large mass medium. There's a lot of people using it, but it's not very specialized in any way.

Paige Beal: Assistant Professor, Marketing & Advertising, Point Park University

Being able to integrate it within the entire media plan.

Guido D'Elia: Partner, Mind Over Media

Understanding what works and what doesn't work and where you stand within it. People are certainly active with it. How you can apply it to business is difficult to understand. You need an expert to be able to help you with that. There is no way to figure that out yourself. You need somebody who is in that field, deep into it. It's tricky, but it's there, and it should be taken advantage of in some way.

Dennis Moran: Principal, Dennis Moran Design

How is it relevant? How can it be relevant for a broad swath of corporate clients? How is it relevant in other scenarios? How is it relevant to a Fortune 500 company?

Julie Smith: Principal/President RJW Media

I don't know if social media is a challenge or an opportunity. You have to know the whole e-commerce part of it, and how to find a follower and how to turn that into a conversion point, or turn that into a benefit or a sale. You have to know how to do something with them now that you have them so that you can turn it into an action.

Saul Markowitz: President, Markowitz Communications

It's not just about Twitter and Facebook. Look, at 47 years old, I have young people teaching me this stuff right now. I think it's the wave of the future, and I think we need to deal with it, but we also need to know what else is out there.

Discussion Questions

1. Do you agree with our panelists' analysis of the challenges in public relations, advertising, marketing, and social media? Address one at a time. Why or why not? What challenges do you see?

2. Do you trust public relations and advertising? Share a story about why or why not.

3. D'Elia said that, with regard to public relations, most audiences start with the thought "This is going to be spun." How do we, as communicators, overcome this immediate skepticism of our messages?

4. Social media looks like a beacon of hope, but will it just become another spin zone lacking credibility? Can we prevent that? How?

5. Should every company and product use social media? Why or why not?

6. Popovic said that the biggest challenge in social media is deciding how to use it for business. What about social media makes its application more challenging than traditional marketing vehicles? Knowing those challenges, is social media still a worthwhile tool for marketers? Why or why not?

7. How can we measure the return on investment (ROI) for social media, if we can at all?

8. Many of our panelists identified marketing "clutter" or "noise" as a significant challenge. Do you agree? If so, how do we eliminate it or cut through it?

Join the Conversation

Scan the QR codes from this section to watch the video for each question, then read the comments shared by others in our community. Add your thoughts to join our conversation.

Q10 | What is the biggest challenge in Public Relations?

Q11 | What is the biggest challenge in Advertising?

Q12 | What is the biggest challenge in Marketing?

Q13 | What is the biggest challenge in Social Media?

Kevin Popović and Saul Markowitz discuss contributors scheduled to appear.
Photo courtesy of Jack Wolf.

Chapter 05 | Creative Challenges

Introduction

In the previous chapter we discussed how distrust for advertising and public relations presented a challenge for communications professionals, but when we asked our panelists about challenges specific to media, the conversation was more about execution and viability of the medium rather than whether or not audiences trusted the messages contained within those mediums.

For communications, the growth of the Internet and all things mobile has created a slew of new opportunities, but those opportunities have not come without growing pains. Newspaper readership and advertising revenue are dropping (Perez-Pena, 2008). Magazine subscriptions are down. And television is flailing wildly to keep services like Hulu and DVR from pillaging their advertising revenue as its overall viewership continues to decline (Pew Research Center, 2011). The Internet has changed the way we consume content, and traditional media seems unsure of its place in a world where most people go online for news and articles and prefer to record their favorite shows to watch later (Center for the Digital Future, 2012). This paradigm shift has many in our industry proclaiming that print is dead and that television is dying. Others are hopeful that traditional media can reinvent itself, and some are fully confident that newspapers, magazines, and television will evolve and thrive in a digital world.

Even our panelists are in disagreement as to the future of traditional media, but they agree that if traditional media is to survive, it must adapt.

The Walls Have Fallen

Because of the Internet, physical boundaries have become less relevant. This has been a boon for communication—more people can connect with each other than ever before—but it has created challenges for our industry that are not unique to media alone. Where traditional media, like local newspapers and magazines, is losing a battle for readership against national and international websites, communications professionals are competing against outsourcing, crowdsourcing, and insourcing, all of which are less costly alternatives to hiring an agency or a freelance professional for design or for multimedia development.

Crowdsourcing, the act of outsourcing work or tasks to a large number of people, was made possible by the Internet, and its power has been used to make websites like e-Lance and iStock great successes. For our industry, however, crowdsourcing is a threat to the way that we do business. Though crowdsourcing can take many forms, work in the form of contests is growing in popularity. A business posts that they need a task completed, like a logo designed, and the winning submission receives a predetermined amount of money. The result: hundreds or thousands of designers from around the world sending in graphics with the hopes that their work is selected. If they win, they are paid. If not, that work was wasted effort. Multiple websites have emerged to facilitate the crowdsourcing process, and they are thriving.

Freelancer.com is one such site, and their CEO, Matt Barrie, says that he wants to turn his site into the "eBay of jobs." Barrie, in an interview with Wired, says, "If a design contest ran for a logo with a prize of $10,000, no one would have a problem with it. But what a lot of these designers don't realize is that the other five billion people in the world live on somewhere around $8 per day or less, which means that design competitions for $250 or $300 represent a month's wage. You can complain about it as much as you want, but these are free market forces" (Solon, 2012).

That's what competition has become. An agency in New York is now competing with designers in India and in Sri Lanka, which is to say that crowdsourcing often means outsourcing. Communicators are competing on quality and price with, well, everyone.

In 2010, Gap Clothing announced that it would crowdsource the design of its new brand identity after the reception of its in-house attempt was poor. Richard Grefé, the Executive Director for the American Institute of Graphic Arts (AIGA), immediately wrote a letter to Gap managers and executives, urging them to reconsider.

He wrote, "[By crowdsourcing], clients risk compromised quality. Little time, energy and thought can go into speculative work, which precludes the most important element of most design projects-the research, thoughtful consideration of alternatives, and development and testing of prototype designs. Designers risk being taken advantage of. Some clients may see this as a way to get free work; it also diminishes the true economic value of the contribution designers make toward client's objectives."

Grefé's position on crowdsourcing and his opinions on the importance of research and thoughtful design echo the opinions espoused by our panelists in this chapter and in previous chapters. Communications is both an art and a science. It requires a great deal of creativity, but in most cases, that creativity is fueled by research that provides context and justification for creative decisions and communications strategies. In the crowdsourcing model, research may be ignored completely, but the reduced costs associated with crowdsourcing and outsourcing are incredibly tempting, especially in hyper-competitive markets and an economy where budgets are ever-shrinking.

Barrie argues that good design for websites and device interfaces is still incredibly important, and that crowdsourcing cannot reliably serve these needs (Solon, 2012). On this topic, Barrie says, "These can make the difference between a business that peters out and dies and one that becomes a billion dollar company. That's where our designers should head towards, rather than designing $100 logos."

At the same time, however, research has found that highly specialized tasks may be impossible to effectively crowdsource, primarily because crowdsourcing cannot consistently connect tasks to the appropriate expert workers (Ranade & Varshney, 2012). The expert workers may not be present in the talent pool and unskilled workers may be polluting the talent pool, reducing the overall quality of the crowdsourced performance. On this point, Barrie, Grefé, and the research are in total agreement: highly specialized tasks that require the experience and expertise of highly skilled professionals are not fit for crowdsourcing (Ipeirotis et al, 2010).

Further complicating our industry is the rise of "do it yourselfers." In Chapter Three, Jack Wolf remarked that the role of the professional photographer has "diminished" because of easy-to-use point-and-click digital cameras easy and to use apps like Instagram. Photography does not face this challenge alone, though. iMovie and Windows Movie Maker make video editing accessible for amateurs. GarageBand does the same for musicians, and GIMP does the same for graphic designers. Web designers, however, are not at all surprised by these developments. They have always had to compete with Dream Waver, free template designers, and the boss's kid nephew that knows some HTML.

Our panelists would likely agree that accessible tools are not inherently negative, but they present a challenge similar to that of crowdsourcing: some tasks are best suited for highly skilled, highly experienced professionals. If a client is unconvinced of this fact, a professional could find it difficult to justify the asking price of their services and thus lose business.

Businesses choosing to pursue the cost-effective alternatives to hiring experts, whether through crowdsourcing or through a low-cost "do it yourselfer," could be the reason that we are seeing clunky or ineffective design being implemented in a variety of markets, as our panelists noted, but at the very least, these findings suggest that professionals in our industry should strive to perform at the highest level possible and dedicate effort to demonstrating that value to clients, both through education and through the success of current clients.

The Rate of Change

Technology and the Internet are two forces that have changed our industry, and we have touched on many other technologies and services that have created new opportunities and new challenges, from social media to software to mobile devices. Many of our panelists identified these developments as both positive and negative. On the one hand, we have more vehicles to leverage to share and deliver messages to target audiences, and in many cases we can now make those messages more meaningful and engaging because of the new technology available to us, but we are also now faced with having to adapt quickly to changes. And the advancement of technology shows no signs of slowing.

According to the futurist Ray Kurzweil (2000), the rate that humankind is acquiring knowledge and advancing technology is exponential. The wheel is spinning faster and faster with each new discovery and each new improvement such that the next 100 years of advancement will be equivalent to the last 20,000 years, and that rate will continue to accelerate. Though many of Kurzweil's other views and predictions are controversial, his analysis of current trends has been widely accepted and reflects the opinions of our panelists. The hastening advancement of technology has made communications technology more accessible, combining technologies that used to cost thousands of dollars separately into singular devices. At the same time, the exponential change that Kurzweil describes has fractured communications channels. Where communicators once relied on three major television networks for delivering messages, we now have thousands of television channels, millions of websites, thousands of apps. Convergence presents a challenge now and in the future, and we discuss it in greater depth later on.

The ability to adapt and the ability to continue learning are important skills now, and it seems that they will be even more important with each passing day. How we do business is changing. The role of media is changing. The multimedia that we develop and the tools that we use to develop it are changing and so is the production process. And the Internet is both a catalyst for and affected by these changes.

An Exponential 20 Years

Communications has changed dramatically in the past 20 years, and creative has changed as well. Our panelists have identified the challenges, opportunities, and uncertainties spawned by this development. Though the immediate solutions to these challenges may not be clear, being aware of the forces shifting our landscape will better prepare us for the future as we evolve as an industry and as individuals.

Q14 | What is the biggest challenge in Media?

Dennis Moran: Principal, Dennis Moran Design

Understanding human beings. Again, it's back to that whole idea of really understanding who you are talking to.

Michael Hills: Vice President/General Manager, Comcast Spotlight

I don't know if we've spent enough time thinking really hard about what the message is that we're creating. We spend more time thinking about how we get it out there and how we measure it. Measurement is fine, but you've got to spend an equal amount in both the art and the science.

Rob Deaner: Founder/Composer, Market Street Sound

The biggest challenge in media and print and all the different mediums is that there is so much clutter. There are so many different avenues. There are so many different places to focus your attention on deciding those ratios and getting your message out. It's a difficult challenge.

Jack Wolf: Commercial Photographer, Wolf Photography

They're on their way out, so I guess their biggest challenge is being cheaper because no one is going to use them anymore. You go to get your newspaper today, and you think there's been a mistake. It's thin. Sunday's newspaper is a lot of advertising and just a little newspaper. If you ever see anybody under 30 reading a newspaper, something's wrong. Young people don't do it, so newspapers have to figure out how to get that audience. And TV commercials have to quit putting type on the TV commercials that's really small. You can't read it, and it doesn't communicate. You have to figure out how you're going to get the pie because the pie is all going to the Internet.

Rick Landesberg: Principal, Landesberg Design

To create a culture where all media has equivalent strength. In other words, where the power of each form of media is allowed to realize itself.

Guido D'Elia: Partner, Mind Over Media

Saturation is an issue, and fragmentation is an issue. And again, people are just jaded. There is so much of it that each generation is untouchable. We are going around on the outside to try and communicate to people, and the younger they are, the more you need to go around it and not directly to it.

Julie Smith: Principal/President RJW Media

Media fragmentation. It's the choices that we have as media planners and buyers knowing how to target our customers, knowing when they're engaged with the options that are out there, so that we can make wise media recommendations for them. I also see a challenge when clients' budgets are cut or when they stay the same. To get more for our clients, especially at a time when there are so many vehicles out there, is difficult. Reaching a customer is starting to cost more because it's so fragmented.

Chauncey Smith: Chief Sales and Marketing Director, ScienceMedia

Print is dead. If I'm a print guy, that's a tough place to be. I think there's a lot of opportunity and that's being able to reach more highly defined user segments through social media and permission marketing if you will. It offers an awful lot of opportunity to be able to connect with people on a more granular level than typical broadcast media has permitted.

Kevin Popović: Founder of Ideahaus

The challenge with traditional media is staying relevant. TV has its challenges with trying to retain viewers, and it's a business. If the advertising dollars aren't there, they can't have a great show. If you don't have a great show, you aren't going to have the viewers that watch the advertising. The evil cycle. We've been saying print is dead for years. I hope that print learns how to reinvent itself. I think its clock is ticking though. Radio is the same thing. ITunes is kicking the hell out of traditional radio in advertising, and I'm just not sure what they're going to do about that.

When you look at traditional media, it is a broken model. It's outdated technology if you will. The way that it used to work just doesn't fly anymore. The technology and the medium and those channels exist, but the business model by which they're involving advertisers it's just outdated. There's got to be a smarter way to use all that technology and that capability to get in front of all those people.

Brian Bronaugh: President/Executive Creative Director, Mullen – Pittsburgh

The news of their death is greatly premature. I think that every time that something new comes along, "Well, that's the end of this." We've still got radio, and we still have television. Those things will obviously continue to change. The iPad announcement was interesting to see how that may extend some of the shelf life of some of these printed publications as well, but I think the challenge is to say that we're not dead. We're viable, and there's a way that you can utilize us to help tell that whole story.

Mike Lee: Founder/Executive Producer, Studious One
Bankruptcy. They are highly invested in antiquated equipment, which they've got to do something with.

Bill Flanagan: Executive Vice President, Corporate Relations, Allegheny Conference
The business model. How do you make money doing it? The more traditional

you are, the bigger the question is. To me, the biggest challenge for newspapers, traditional television, or some online media is how do we pay for quality production and for quality information when the market is so fragmented that there are millions of websites and a page for everyone in the world? I'm not sure I understand where the great content is going to come from in the future when it's divvied up into so many tiny little audiences.

Raelin Sawka Musuraca: Digital Strategist
If we keep defining media in these little buckets, we're going to hamper ourselves as a discipline, and I'm not just saying this because I'm a digital strategist. It's all going to converge. The pipe that brings it into your house—the FiOS pipe that brings the TV, the Internet, and the telephone into your house—is basically the same pipe, the same data. It just puts it on different devices that are comfortable to us. There's really no need to do it from a technology point of view. It's for our own comfort. Those will come together. As industry professionals, we're not ready for that. I know way too many people that are TV broadcast specialists and just don't understand what that means when you're going to put it in a different environment like YouTube. We need to be able to understand when those converge and be ready for it.

Glenn Przyborski: Director/Cinematographer, Przyborski Productions
Finding a way to pay for the media. That seems to be it right now. With the economy lagging back a little bit, I know clients have less money to spend, and that's helped us a little bit with some clients because they can't run to New York or do the shoot in Los Angeles. Today with the proliferation of digital and all the other things, people are accepting that there are talented people all around the country. We frequently bid against people I've never even heard of, and then we look at their reel and go "Wow, they're not bad." It's a wakeup call when you see something out of the middle of Ohio that you never heard of and you look at their reel and say, "They're not bad. I might consider using them too."

Paige Beal: Assistant Professor, Marketing & Advertising, Point Park University
Being able to embrace new media.

Don Decker: Regional Sales, Comcast Spotlight
Evolving to the client's need. A lot of clients are looking to grow their business in interactive areas, rightly so at this point, but keeping it well balanced

with traditional media will help support the foundation of their business.

Roy Cheran: Director of Business Development, Mind Over Media
What's effective and what's useless?

Saul Markowitz: President, Markowitz Communications
All those people, outdoor and I think of TV especially: "Hey, it's 2010, everyone." Think about it. They have to catch up. These people really need to catch up.

David Sladack: VP & Group Account Strategy Director, Brunner Advertising
The biggest challenge in traditional media is that traditionally it was all about spots and dots and making sure you have a presence. You have to do a lot more than that today. You actually have to have a real role there in the beginning and an engaging, interactive role with the media that you're purchasing.

Michael Lotenero: Designer/Artist, Michael Lotenero Art + Design
I don't know if they even have any challenges. It just seems like they're having a good time, especially with the way they can manipulate politics and people. It's fun to watch.

Q15 | What is the biggest challenge in Design?

Roy Cheran: Director of Business Development, Mind Over Media
Subjectivity.

Mike Lee: Founder/Executive Producer, Studious One
Being original.

Don Decker: Regional Sales, Comcast Spotlight
Not over designing.

Saul Markowitz: President, Markowitz Communications
People over design things sometimes, and they need to chill out.

Rick Landesberg: Principal, Landesberg Design
Clarity.

Bill Flanagan: Executive Vice President, Corporate Relations, Allegheny Conference

The former CEO of Ford Motor Company said he wanted to make a product that would surprise and delight the customer, and that's always struck me. To me, the designer needs to ask him or herself the question, "What is there about this product that I've created that will surprise and delight the customer?" If you've got that in your head, you're probably on the track to a winner.

Dennis Moran: Principal, Dennis Moran Design

It's one of defining what design is. The biggest challenge is getting a broad audience to understand that design is not an add-on. Design is not something you put on after you've done all the thinking. It's not the decoration. It's not the rearrangement. It's an intellectual process that really has the potential to improve just about anything that takes a visible form.

Brian Bronaugh: President/Executive Creative Director, Mullen – Pittsburgh

That so much of it is so goddamn bad right now. Anytime you have a seat change in technology—do you remember when we got desktop publishing? How awful typography was and how awful page layout was? There's a similarity now. We call MP3 good enough. It's whatever you can get out quickly as opposed to aesthetically. That'll catch up. That train will come, but right now the challenge is to get people who are better designers in these new mediums.

David Sladack: VP & Group Account Strategy Director, Brunner Advertising
The biggest challenge is designing for a new mobile world coming up.

Raelin Sawka Musuraca: Digital Strategist
The biggest challenge in design is usability. A really good designer knows how to make something that looks great and is very usable, and I am not just talking about the digital world. I could mean the usability of a print piece or a door. Oftentimes we get caught up with how pretty something is and don't think about the functionality. Usability is the real challenge.

Michael Lotenero: Designer/Artist, Michael Lotenero Art + Design

The biggest challenge in marketing is communicating with design, and the biggest challenge in design is communicating with marketing. I don't think that we all talk. We don't speak the same language.

The firms I've worked in, everybody's got their own agendas, and everybody's got their own thing to do. No one really talks and sits down at the same table and hammers out a great project all the time. It's a tough, tough thing to do. Everybody's got their egos. If we talk about communication internally, if design and marketing want to communicate, we'll have better projects and outcomes.

Paige Beal: Assistant Professor, Marketing & Advertising, Point Park University
I am challenged in design, so it's hard for me to answer without understanding that. At the same time, it's like marketing. Design has to speak to the target.

Guido D'Elia: Partner, Mind Over Media

Sticking to the target and making sure that it's the same premise. Make sure that you are designing from the back end, from the user's point of view and what they need.

Michael Hills: Vice President/General Manager, Comcast Spotlight

Cost versus really good design. We have tried to commoditize design the way we have in some extent to buying media, and you cannot commoditize design. If you're trying to replace great design with inexpensive design, good luck.

Chauncey Smith: Chief Sales and Marketing Director, ScienceMedia

In design, it's the do-it-yourself craze. Things like Adobe Captivate make it very simple for lay people with limited programming knowledge to develop fairly simplistic but effective communications. That will limit the opportunity for agencies and custom shops like mine to be able to go in and do that work for them.

Kevin Popović: Founder of Ideahaus

The biggest challenge in design is trying to demonstrate your return on investment. I'm a huge fan of design. I have a design background. I continue to offer design services, but I see a commoditization of design with the advent of things like istockphoto.com where you don't have to hire a great photographer and go through the whole process. You can put in a couple keywords and find 10,000 things that photographers–experienced and inexperienced–have submitted as stock, and you can get it for pennies on the dollar.

You also see things like crowdsourcing and sites like E-Lance where a client will come on and say, "Hey, I need a logo. I have 250 bucks. Get it submitted by Thursday, and I'll pick the one I like and then if I like yours, you'll get paid." That's a problem for designers. I'm not sure what we're going to do about it, but it's a problem.

Jack Wolf: Commercial Photographer, Wolf Photography

You ever go to a design firm? They sit around and have focus groups and then they think about it, and they'll get back to you in a week. A logo. Do you know now that you can go on Logo Care, www.logocare.com, and for $259 you can get unlimited logos sent to your house? You can go to a design firm and a week later they'll be putting the butterfly over the letter

T, and eventually you'll get around to having a logo. The designers, they have to get with it, man. It's a logo.

Q16 | What is the biggest challenge in Multimedia?

Raelin Sawka Musuraca: Digital Strategist
Multi what? Isn't it dead?

Mike Lee: Founder/Executive Producer, Studious One
Video.

Don Decker: Regional Sales, Comcast Spotlight
Targetablility.

Chauncey Smith: Chief Sales and Marketing Director, ScienceMedia
Getting it small enough to fit in a mobile application.

David Sladack: VP & Group Account Strategy Director, Brunner Advertising
I think the biggest challenge is engagement without being obtrusive.

Rick Landesberg: Principal, Landesberg Design
Staying focused on the subject. To let the message ring out over bells and whistles. Bells and whistles at the service of message.

Bill Flanagan: Executive Vice President, Corporate Relations, Allegheny Conference
The biggest challenge: overdoing it and having so many bells and whistles that get in the way of your message and your communication actually becomes less effective.

Saul Markowitz: President, Markowitz Communications
People just don't know really how to do it yet. Study a little bit more before you start doing it.

Michael Hills: Vice President/General Manager, Comcast Spotlight
That the multi is bigger. There's more of it.

Brian Bronaugh: President/Executive Creative Director, Mullen – Pittsburgh
There hasn't been a consistent workflow for them. We've had Flash people. We've had multimedia people. There are times when they're completely

overwhelmed. There are times when they're sitting around waiting. We need to have people who can be plugged into various different channels, so we're looking for very hybrid folks that can do Flash, that can do multimedia, but that can also design and can also shoot and edit for us as well.

Paige Beal: Assistant Professor, Marketing & Advertising, Point Park University
The biggest challenge in multimedia is really the understanding of the ability to use all of it. It's a body of knowledge issue, so much to know, so little time to know it and employ it.

Guido D'Elia: Partner, Mind Over Media

Keeping current with what's out there and not jumping around too much to whatever is the latest or that can take you down the wrong path. It's good and bad that there is a lot of new stuff out there constantly, but you've got to be able to measure what's right for you and your client.

Dennis Moran: Principal, Dennis Moran Design
Making it relevant. Making sure it doesn't become just about design, that it's not just decoration and being cute, that it's not just effect, that there's content and meaning to it. There's a reason why you use that media.

Julie Smith: Principal/President RJW Media
Two things. I think there are so many options. There are so many websites. When we're looking to place an online campaign for a client, there are a lot of options, and publishers are creating more opportunity, so

we're just going to see more and more. It's trial and error of knowing what options to best recommend for the client.

Another challenge would be that clients aren't defining their objectives when wanting to do an advertising campaign. They don't have a clear goal or objective in mind that will allow us to measure success.

Rob Deaner: Founder/Composer, Market Street Sound
From my perspective, the biggest problem in multimedia is formatting. There are so many different formats and so little standardization. It's really hard to effectively collaborate.

Glenn Przyborski: Director/Cinematographer, Przyborski Productions
To have a product that works universally among all these different medium forms because everything we do today is high definition, but typically it ends up being some little QuickTime movie on the Internet. It has to translate to that, which means if you know that ahead of time you're going to shoot it a certain way, where things are closer and tighter. That's a challenge but it's something that you just sort of expect.

Michael Lotenero: Designer/Artist, Michael Lotenero Art + Design
I'll talk to people, like my brother-in-law, who's an airplane pilot, and he says, "Oh, I'm playing around with Flash this weekend." And I'm like, "Really?" People that never had access to these tools have access to these tools now. The playing field has been leveled in terms of who can make their own content. It's going to be interesting to see in the next 10 years what that looks like.

Q17 | What is the biggest challenge in Internet Development?

Roy Cheran: Director of Business Development, Mind Over Media
Technology over substance.

Brian Bronaugh: President/Executive Creative Director, Mullen – Pittsburgh
What kind of information we're willing to share, which has to do with GPS and sensor technology, and the American idea of privacy versus a global idea of privacy. The Europeans treat it as their right, and we sort of treat

it as a consumer protection free speech thing that we've grown up with. It's different from what the Europeans have. From a digital perspective, how to deal with private information and how we share it is the biggest challenge going.

Rick Landesberg: Principal, Landesberg Design

Retaining expressiveness while displaying information clearly.

Chauncey Smith: Chief Sales and Marketing Director, ScienceMedia

Prioritization. It's a playground out there. There are an awful lot of things that are both emerging and developing. Mobile, to me, is the one that's most interesting, because with the explosion of the iPhone and smart phones, there are certainly going to be opportunities to reach key target audiences through those devices. That challenge, to me, offers a lot of upside.

Rob Deaner: Founder/Composer, Market Street Sound

The biggest challenge in website development that I see as a non-developer, as a user, is efficiency, ease of use. We as humans have a tendency to over-design and make things more complicated than they need to be. Technology has been a blessing for me. It's huge. It's hugely benefited my processes. At the same time, certain things take a lot longer than they used to.

Don Decker: Regional Sales, Comcast Spotlight

Not making it too complicated. Making it easy for the user getting to the website. When they get on, making it where they can navigate around, find what they're looking for, and not have to do a bunch of searches. A well-designed site, one that users can get on and locate the information they want, is key.

Saul Markowitz: President, Markowitz Communications

A few years ago, I would say too much Flash. People sometimes over Flash things. It's like that's enough already. I'm getting a seizure. Cut it out. I think at this moment in web design: simplify it a little bit.

Paige Beal: Assistant Professor, Marketing & Advertising, Point Park University
Usability. That's a constant. Designers, developers, somewhere in between— someone needs to be talking usability, and more often than not that's what's missing.

Glenn Przyborski: Director/Cinematographer, Przyborski Productions
A lot of people make sites that are esoteric but not functional. When I go to a site, I like to see who this person is that I'm going to call and some background on him or whatever. A lot of sites are visually interesting but convey nothing to me.

Jack Wolf: Commercial Photographer, Wolf Photography
Getting all that clutter off the screen. Did you ever go to a good photographer's website? Name, clients, address, contact, beautiful pictures. Go to Go-Daddy.com. Do you know what GoDaddy.com is? Danica Patrick flashing

up here, 17 things that are on sale over here, the reason why you should do it down here, and the little box that says questions. How do you get by that? It's simplicity. It's got to be simple. Really simple.

Guido D'Elia: Partner, Mind Over Media
Time to get it done. So many things are changing in that arena that keeping up with what's the latest and how to do it and how to arrive at it is probably the biggest challenge. There are so many specialists and so many narrow niches in there that it's really difficult to get across-the-board coverage within an organization.

Bill Flanagan: Executive Vice President, Corporate Relations, Allegheny Conference
Just trying to keep up with it. Social media is a real conundrum for a lot of folks. I don't know, frankly, how much money to invest in it or how much time to put into it because I know what the results are in traditional media. I still don't really understand what can be accomplished there, and it's all moving so fast. It's just hard to keep up with.

David Sladack: VP & Group Account Strategy Director, Brunner Advertising
Keeping things relevant and frequently changing them.

Michael Lotenero: Designer/Artist, Michael Lotenero Art + Design
Keeping the content fast and keeping it available. I like the idea of people being able to change things on the fly and being able to update their status. I know some of those things might be weird for people, but it's kind of strange because it seems like our generation is really all over Facebook. Things get labeled right off the bat, and it's like, wow, you can take ownership of a technology and enjoy it. It's the Wild West out there with that.

Kevin Popović: Founder of Ideahaus
The Internet is a wonderful thing, and there are a lot of opportunities. The challenge is that there are sometimes too many opportunities. Whether it's the technology that you build the site on or worrying if your prospect has the right browser and plug-in, and bandwidth to deliver the things to deliver these things - I think that's a challenge. I think the Internet will settle itself down over time with some more standardization as some of these things succeed more than others, but that's the challenge with Internet development: too many choices.

Michael Hills: Vice President/General Manager, Comcast Spotlight

The pace at which change is happening. Internet itself is one thing. Websites are clearly not new media anymore. The problem is less about that and more about how many different options there are. There are dozens and dozens of options to communicate to people through mobile media, for example. And they change so quickly. Again, I don't think people can keep up with it.

Julie Smith: Principal/President RJW Media

There's still growth. I still think there's a lot to learn. The biggest challenge is people getting behind it and really seeing the benefit of it and getting involved and engaged in it.

Raelin Sawka Musuraca: Digital Strategist

Being out over your skis. The Internet and web development were always far out ahead of the curve. We don't know if something is going to work or not, whereas broadcast and print have been traditional. You know how to print something. It's not going to go wrong. Now, we are constantly living in a state of being out over our skis, and for some people that's very uncomfortable. For some people, you might not hit the deadline they want, but you can't hold back. You got to be out there. You got to be pushing it to the edge. You're never going to accomplish what you need to if you don't.

Q18 | What is the biggest challenge in Production?

Don Decker: Regional Sales, Comcast Spotlight
Getting it done timely.

Roy Cheran: Director of Business Development, Mind Over Media
Style and execution.

Paige Beal: Assistant Professor, Marketing & Advertising, Point Park University
The lack of appreciation for quality and the emphasis on speed.

Saul Markowitz: President, Markowitz Communications
Sometimes people just over-produce it, and we need to focus in on the people that really know what they're doing when it comes to post-production.

Chauncey Smith: Chief Sales and Marketing Director, ScienceMedia
There's an awful lot of do-it-yourself nature to folks, certainly when times are tough, and obviously we are in tough economic times here at the moment. Being able to try and carve out a little of the production to in-house or in-source it, if you will, versus working outside is probably a downward pressure that the production folks are feeling.

Michael Hills: Vice President/General Manager, Comcast Spotlight
There are so many options for production now. You can do inexpensive production using tools on your Mac at home, and there are a lot of folks doing it. Some of them do it great, and some of them don't, so the balance of accessibility and inexpensive access to production is at one time a great opportunity, and it's also a real challenge.

David Sladack: VP & Group Account Strategy Director, Brunner Advertising
The biggest challenge in production is really preparing for a digital world. You have to price yourself and have timing that fits the needs of the digital world.

Rob Deaner: Founder/Composer, Market Street Sound
The biggest challenge in production are the shrinking budgets with high expectations. Every week it's how do we do for $10,000 what should cost $300,000? It happens more and more. Because of that, quality and

consistency suffer, and therefore the message suffers.

Glenn Przyborski: Director/Cinematographer, Przyborski Productions

I shot tons of film, TV ads. I don't want to say that film is a dead entity, but I've gotten to the point where I do not prefer the look of film over really well-done digital television. We have done commercials where we did a test shot of two different things, one digitally and one shot on 35. The client preferred the digital look over the 35, so it isn't necessarily everyone trying to emulate film anymore. The new technology and options are a challenge, but if I were them I'd worry about the communications rather than the exact type of camera.

Mike Lee: Founder/Executive Producer, Studious One

YouTube. Accessible video production to the common person. Everyone thinks they can be the next Scorsese. You're really still a dude with a flip phone camera.

Bill Flanagan: Executive Vice President, Corporate Relations, Allegheny Conference

One of the challenges I see is YouTube. It's redefining what quality production is. I come from a very traditional television environment where you do things by the book, and all bets seem to be off. So what is quality anymore when you're talking production, and how do you really know? I assume it comes down to the audience, but it's a real challenge. It has to be for everybody involved.

Guido D'Elia: Partner, Mind Over Media

The price of entry into production is so low these days, and there are so many talented people. A lot of them think they can do it. It's almost like still photography. Everyone has a camera, and so it becomes a matter of, "why do I need to hire someone?" That's come into the video world, and to some degree, to building websites. It's commoditizing the marketplace, so we'll just have to see how that turns out.

Brian Bronaugh: President/Executive Creative Director, Mullen – Pittsburgh
The biggest challenge for folks in the production area is that we (agencies) have taken over a lot of the production. Agencies can do a lot of work in house now, and as revenue streams continue to get tighter and tighter, we're always looking for ways to increase our profit margin, so the challenge is with technology and the way it's advanced. How do production companies partner with agencies so that we both get value out of the equation?

Discussion Questions

1. How can traditional media, like newspapers, magazines, and television, evolve to survive and thrive in a digital world?

2. Is crowdsourcing good or bad for the communications industry? How can we succeed in spite of it?

3. Barrie argues that communications professionals should focus on the high-level tasks rather than the small tasks that can be crowdsourced. Is this possible for the industry as a whole? Why or why not? How will it change our industry?

4. What are the challenges that you see in design? How can we overcome them?

5. Beal said that "design has to speak to the target." What does she mean by that?

6. What are the challenges that you see in multimedia and production? How can we overcome them?

7. According to Popovic, the current television model is broken. He said, "The technology and the medium and those channels exist, but the business model by which they're involving advertisers it's just outdated. There's got to be a smarter way to use all that technology and that capability to get in front of all those people." Do you agree? Is there a smarter way? What is it?

8. What is the best strategy for keeping up with new advances in technology, on and offline? How do we keep from being overwhelmed by every new start-up and program?

9. Is it good or bad that more people are exploring photography, design, multimedia, and production as hobbies? How will this change the industry, and can we use those changes to our advantage?

Join the Conversation

Scan the QR codes from this section to watch the video for each question, then read the comments shared by others in our community. Add your thoughts to join our conversation.

Q14 | What is the biggest challenge in Media?

Q15 | What is the biggest challenge in Design?

Q16 | What is the biggest challenge in Multimedia?

Q17 | What is the biggest challenge in Internet Development?

Q18 | What is the biggest challenge in Production?

Kevin Popović and Michael Lotenero reminisce about starting careers 20 years prior. Photo courtesy of Jack Wolf.

Chapter 06 | Reflections and Predictions

Introduction

In 1989, James Carey, a highly regarded and respected communications theorist, argued that the telegraph's ability to transmit messages over great distances almost instantaneously revolutionized communications and culture. Economics changed. Politics changed. Even the style of prose changed—shorter, simpler, a style born of a communication medium defined by brevity. While inventions like the telegraph undoubtedly bring about significant change, Carey asserted, they may not necessarily make the world better. He said that the telegraph made business less personal, that face-to-face communication fell out of favor, and that the new model—lacking personal relationships—was more monopolistic and expanded the divide between the "haves" and the "have nots."

Though the telegraph changed communications, it did not improve society or better the human condition in Carey's mind. Neither did electricity, and neither did the Internet. To Carey, technology is not the facilitator of positive change. Despite its supposed potential, humans themselves must make a change in order for technology to truly make a difference. In this way, Carey's writing echoes a sentiment once expressed by Edward R. Murrow, a famous American journalist: "The newest computer can merely compound, at speed, the oldest problem in the relations between human beings, and in the end the communicator will be confronted with the old problem, of what to say and how to say it."

Many of our panelists seem to disagree with Carey's position, and they are not alone. Carey's work is both influential and controversial, the subject of many classroom debates and the inspiration for continued research for academics worldwide. Unlike Carey, our panelists see the Internet and social media and mobile technology as a means of connecting people, but almost all of our panelists seem to agree that no matter what medium lies between us and our audience, we are ultimately, as Murrow suggested, humans connecting with humans, a fact that may have been forgotten by our predecessors in some instances that could be remembered as we explore the new developments in technology and culture in the next 20 years.

Convergence

Media convergence is an extension of the idea of technological convergence, which is a phenomenon where separate technologies gradually approach performing more and more similar tasks (Jenkins, 2004). In terms of communications and media, convergence is best described by example. At one point, television, telephones, newspapers, and mail existed as separate entities. Now, these communication tools have converged into singular mobile devices. In a way, convergence is an extension of the world-flattening aspect of globalization that has been a theme throughout this book, and it touches upon the culture-shifting power of reduced space and time between communicators that Carey describes in his work. More accessibility is a benefit in many ways but a significant challenge in others.

As mobile phones continue to become an extension of ourselves in both a physical and emotional sense, their significance in communication continues to grow as well. Sure you are filming a beautiful car commercial, but how will it look and load on a smart phone? Can you incorporate social media? How can you make the copy search engine optimized? Can you find some bloggers that would write about the video and share it with their audiences?

Very rarely are we operating in a singular channel in this age of convergence, despite our accessing these channels from a single device. The more that we spend our lives online as well as offline, the more plentiful our digital footprints become. Amazon recommends books specific to your tastes based on your purchase history, your browsing history, and your review history. Netflix does the same with movies. Google does the same with advertising. In fact, recommending products based on a customer's history is so commonplace now that it feels wholly unremarkable, but the science behind these systems is quite incredible (Goff, 2011).

Target, a large retailer chain, set out to convert new mothers to loyal customers (Duhigg, 2012). Through research, they learned that the life change of having a child creates a brief period of flux, a period where women will leave behind old brand loyalties and radically change their shopping habits. This was not old news to marketers. Companies had been using birth registries to send new mothers advertisements and promotional offers for years, but Target wanted to find a way to identify expecting mothers through purchasing decisions. If it was possible, Target could contact the soon-to-be parents well before the competition and increase its chances of converting new lifetime customers.

The result: a Minneapolis man stormed into his local Target and demanded to know why the company was encouraging his high school daughter to buy cribs and bibs and formula. It turned out that she was already pregnant and had not told him yet, but Target knew.

Some of our panelists suggest that direct marketing will reach science fiction proportions, where computers in stores will check your status updates and cross reference your purchasing history and ping you with ads specific to you when you walk through the door. Given the Target anecdote and current convergence trends, a world rife with Minority Report advertising does not seem that outlandish.

The 20 Years Ahead

Convergence was a major topic among our panelists, but few were comfortable making specific predictions as to what the future holds for communications, perhaps rightly so in an industry that has been changing rapidly and in surprising ways. Twitter was a surprise, and even in a culture mostly comfortable to social media, Pinterest too was a surprise. Now these surprises are market forces. Savvy communicators saw their potential and immediately put them to use to spread messages through new but thriving channels. And that may be the single most important theme in this book: learn, adapt, repeat.

Q19 | What is the most significant advancement for communications in the last 20 years?

Roy Cheran: Director of Business Development, Mind Over Media

The last 20 years? That's after the bong was out of the whole picture, right?

I take a little different tack to social media because my thinking is that although many people are gravitating toward social media, there is a convergence of technology and connectivity relative to communications. Socially, physically, and professionally, what can I maintain relative to my network; just physically what can I accomplish and get done? The key thing is that there will always be room for traditional media and always room for new media. It's just a question of who is your audience and where is the herd the largest? And those are the mediums you want to use to communicate to them with.

Guido D'Elia: Partner, Mind Over Media

Technology without a doubt. Technology is driving everything that we do, and it takes all you have to keep up with it. I'm not sure that anybody does keep up with it. A lot of people think they do, but as soon as you think you are keeping up with technology, I guarantee you are not.

Mike Lee: Founder/Executive Producer, Studious One

I know everyone's going to say the web and what not. I think it's compression of data. We started off with Matthew Broderick in War Games with the AT&T Mobile phone on the analog modem, and they were just reading ones and zeros based on tones. High-speed information is limited by the size of the pipe, but what makes those physical pipes even better is better compression. And the algorithms are getting more and more complex so that we can send digital media more efficiently.

Brian Bronaugh: President/Executive Creative Director, Mullen – Pittsburgh
It's got to be the online world and the speed at which bandwidth continues to grow. It's like the wheel. It opened up this plethora of other ways to communicate.

David Sladack: VP & Group Account Strategy Director, Brunner Advertising
In the last 20 years, technology convergence changed the whole dynamic. It's been a paradigm shift in how we communicate and influence people. And not only that, but to be able to just not talk to them but talk with them.

Rob Deaner: Founder/Composer, Market Street Sound
The biggest advance is in immediacy, like cell phones, and the immediacy of connecting people. With the advent of social media, you can start connecting with each other, and through some interaction you can have a common experience where you didn't before. People are getting drawn closer together.

Don Decker: Regional Sales, Comcast Spotlight
Cell phones, for sure. They're ubiquitous. They're everywhere anymore, and that's changed the face of how a lot of people do business and communicate.

Chauncey Smith: Chief Sales and Marketing Director, ScienceMedia
The explosion of cellular phones—whether it's texting, sending images, your calendar, or your smart phone. That's probably been the biggest advancement. In terms of opportunities, how do you leverage that channel to really build a relationship and effectively communicate with your target audience? It's one of the bigger opportunities I see in the marketplace.

Julie Smith: Principal/President RJW Media
The addition of two screens to our world. The cell phone and the computer join the television screen, making what I call the "three screen approach." People are consuming more video than ever these days. They're just doing it on three different channels, through three different avenues: television, computer, and mobile phone.

Glenn Przyborski: Director/Cinematographer, Przyborski Productions
It has to be the computer. Years ago, it used to cost half a million dollars worth of electronics to post-produce something. It used to take a TV camera that was $75,000 and then a whole crew to make something look pretty good. Today, you can buy a simple television camera, high definition, for less than $1000, a nice PowerBook computer, and literally you can produce a network TV show or a network grade TV spot with just those two devices if you have the talent.

Michael Lotenero: Designer/Artist, Michael Lotenero Art + Design
The most obvious answer is computers and the Internet. We're still living in this industrial society where everybody wants you to sit there for eight hours a day and collect your paycheck. We have all these tools that have made our lives so efficient, and we're getting everything done quicker, but they don't want you to take advantage of that. Why can't you work three hours a day and then go home with your kids or go do other stuff? It's kind of ridiculous. It's going to take awhile for the rest of the world to catch up with that model, but once it does it'll be pretty nice.

Saul Markowitz: President, Markowitz Communications
Oh my God, the Internet. No choice about it. You can work anywhere now. I've been traveling around the country doing certain things, and I can still have my base here in Pittsburgh. It wasn't like that 20 years ago. When you were snowed out 20 years ago at home for a week, you were done. This time around, I'm snowed in for a week, and I'm texting my staff. We're emailing each other. We're G-Chatting. It is so easy. It's a real exciting time now to be in communications.

Bill Flanagan: Executive Vice President, Corporate Relations, Allegheny Conference
The last 20 years is the Internet. It's probably as important as the movable type that Gutenberg invented 500 years ago. It's revolutionized the world. To have literally a world of information at your fingertips instantly no matter where you are is changing every single game, and we're seeing it all around us.

Michael Hills: Vice President/General Manager, Comcast Spotlight
Internet, by far, and there is so much that you can do with the Internet that it's not just websites. It's everything you can do on the Internet that has changed everything, not just advertising but the way people do business, the way they live their life, the way they communicate, and certainly the way we market to them. It's an amazing tool.

Rick Landesberg: Principal, Landesberg Design

It's easy to say "Oh, let's talk about the web." The core questions about communications and creativity remain the same. It's hard to talk about the past and the future in terms of what has changed that much. The core questions are the ongoing ones. When we really look at the big picture of what communicating can do in terms of the social fabric, the questions haven't changed. Is Twitter going to solve any of this stuff, you know?

Dennis Moran: Principal, Dennis Moran Design

If you had to look at one single part of it, it's Google. Google is a thin slice of the Internet and I find that, again, I'm just an observer of the human condition. I try to learn about how people think and how they work. Google has become a working method.

Paige Beal: Assistant Professor, Marketing & Advertising, Point Park University

The Internet. There's no doubt about that, but I think most recently Twitter and real-time social media. I don't know what that's going to mean in the future, but I do know that it has absolutely permeated every bit of what we talk about in media.

Kevin Popović: Founder of Ideahaus

The biggest advancement in the last 20 years has to be the Internet. That big-picture item has facilitated so many spin offs and smaller items that have changed the way that people communicate and the way businesses communicate with their customers, no matter who they are.

Raelin Sawka Musuraca: Digital Strategist

As cliché as this sounds, I'm going to say social media. It's the ability for people to talk to each other about brands and to talk to each other about their experiences, whether that's consumer to brand or business to business. Technology is enabling the interaction that's happening real-time on cell phones, on smart phones. There are some really good things that can come out of that, some really bad things as well, but that's going to completely change our industry and what we do as marketing, communications professionals.

Jack Wolf: Commercial Photographer, Wolf Photography

Internet. It's the only thing. Nobody reads books. Nobody reads magazines. The first thing—no, well, the first thing you guys do in the morning, and I wish I was with you—is get up and get on that cell phone. You look to see who did what and who's going where and why are they and where are they? And then you go to your computer. You used to pick up the phone and call somebody. "Hello, you want to go out? How's your mother?" No more.

Q20 | What will impact communications over the next 20 years?

Jack Wolf: Commercial Photographer, Wolf Photography:
The problem with the future is you ever know you never know what's ahead. Yogi Bear said it. He said, "The problem with the future you never know how it's going to turn out." So, I don't know.

Mike Lee: Founder/Executive Producer, Studious One
I believe that it's actually fuel cells and wireless energy which will create devices where you can interact with people 24 hours a day no matter what they are. Now, I'm not just talking about cell phones and things like that. Fuel cells that are independent of wires that can now be places anywhere in the world, giving us another method of communicating with people. It's going to be absolutely revolutionary.

Roy Cheran: Director of Business Development, Mind Over Media
The biggest advancement I see in the next 15 to 20 years will be having the ability to understand what happens when convergence occurs. The early adopters of Facebook and the web and social media and the later adopters will converge and understand that not everybody is going to go this direction, not everyone is going to go that direction. When they begin to fragment at the point of impact, the tools or media used to communicate to those folks could be very disparate in terms of the media choices and selections but can all still be in your target audience, so you have to be nimble and flexible relative to how you develop your communications plan and strategy. Forty years ago with the advent of color television, if you wanted to advertise in a big way and blanket the earth, boom, that was the way to do it. Times have changed and media has changed.

Michael Hills: Vice President/General Manager, Comcast Spotlight
To me it's going to be the convergence of things like the Internet and television. It's a convergence of multiple mediums that's very powerful. In my business it is clearly going to be interactive television. The interactive nature of TV has already started and will continue to grow. Today you can tell your television what you want to watch. You can watch things in video on demand. You can DVR a program and watch it later. Those are the first steps, but ultimately things like being able to press a button and watch a

four-minute video to learn more or go directly to someone's website and learn more after you see a commercial spot will become the norm. That's going to change everything.

Glenn Przyborski: Director/Cinematographer, Przyborski Productions
You're going to see some changes where the television station becomes of less relevance. You'll eventually go on your computer and select the five episodes you might want to watch that night, and they'll come in that way as opposed to an over-the-air television station. The reason I say that is today if you're a news junky, if you're into political news and all that kind of stuff, you go specifically to Fox news or CNBC or one of these providers. You don't necessarily wait around for the six o'clock news on a local TV station. In other words, I don't see where NBC gains anything with the local station. If they can go right to you, and maybe there's some sort of fee that the advertiser pays, why do they need that intermediary in the middle of things?

Rick Landesberg: Principal, Landesberg Design
I have trouble thinking about my garden in the spring. I'm sorry I can't be more responsive than that, but that's really how I feel about it.

Saul Markowitz: President, Markowitz Communications
Online is going to be the hottest still. Over the last five years, with what technology has been like, I think there are some real exciting things about to happen. Doing my field is going to be even easier and more exciting in the next 20 years. I can't wait for it. I'll be doing 3Dish looking interviews with my clients. Seriously. My client will be sitting right here, and we'll beam them into the studio of a news station. When they're done, camera goes off, and they're back where they were before. They won't even need to leave the room.

The only big problem we're going to have when a crisis does come up in PR is that everybody's going to know about it. It's going to be really, really difficult to try to kill off a story in 20 years because there's going to be too many media outlets, too many ways for people to see your story. We're going to have to come up with a way of controlling the PR in a better way.

Kevin Popović: Founder of Ideahaus

What we're going to see in the future is what we saw in Minority Report. This technology where when a person walks into a business there's biometrics that say, "Hey, Kevin has come into our store or he's nearby. We learn from his Facebook profile that he's going on a trip. Perhaps we should sell him a new camera for his trip?" So as he gets to the electronics store, a sales associate says, "Hey, we know you're going on a trip, perhaps you need a new camera?"

As much as that sounds creepy for some people, there's going to be an upside and positive side to that. We'll learn the best way to adopt it through some trial and error, but I'm not so much worried about Big Brother as I am concerned about the return of the customer relationship. As people become comfortable with it and it becomes part of our everyday life, we can return to that customer relationship that we used to have, where the person that was representing the company was looked at as an advocate, as a resource, as an expert in something and made sure that the business and the consumer had a better relationship.

Don Decker: Regional Sales, Comcast Spotlight

Personalized advertising. You're walking by a store, and they say, "Hey, Kevin, come on in. You need a pair of 33-inch waist jeans." They communicate to you when you're walking by a store or send a text message to your phone. Those things are coming. It's just a matter of time when they can launch on a bigger platform to the public.

Raelin Sawka Musuraca: Digital Strategist

It's going to come back and be more personal, be more one to one. Technologies sort of separate us and put us on these computer networks. Computers will become ubiquitous with our lives. They will be things we wear and things that we operate. They're going to be so small, and it'll be back to people and social interaction. That's the way it's going to be, rather than these big devices we use and communicate with.

Michael Lotenero: Designer/Artist, Michael Lotenero Art + Design

It is interesting to see even in the latest natural disasters how quickly we can help people, how quickly people can get engaged in doing that sort of thing. It's encouraging to see how quickly people can network and come together for a cause. I'd like to see more that, of technology being leveraged.

Chauncey Smith: Chief Sales and Marketing Director, ScienceMedia

I expect that the pendulum may swing back a bit toward not technology being the core but relationships and how you build those relationships through communication. Maybe it's not necessarily the technological advancement we've seen over the last 20 year but a deepening of customer intimacy and relationships.

Jack Wolf: Commercial Photographer, Wolf Photography

I think it could be the shoe. Why the shoe? Well, do you remember that TV sitcom *Get Smart*? He talked into it, right? Communication. You're certainly going to be able to take a picture with one soon. You'll be able to blow things up.

David Sladack: VP & Group Account Strategy Director, Brunner Advertising

Over the next five to 10 years, the big advancement is going to be the growth of mobile technology and with that is a continued need to really focus on the individual. Technology will be really, really geared toward solving individual problems and communicating on an individual level, so that means big brands can speak to you now on a one-to-one level on a simple, regular basis.

Julie Smith: Principal/President RJW Media

Mobile is going to take off. It's going to go to the next level, and I think that the computer and the cell phone is going to be one unit. That unit is going to allow us to communicate with the consumer directly and instantaneously.

Bill Flanagan: Executive Vice President, Corporate Relations, Allegheny Conference

I'm fascinated by hand-held devices. The iPod apps and what you can do with a Blackberry—we seem to be on a cusp of that revolution right now. Clearly, there's tens of thousands of apps already available that can do all sorts of things, but just looking back at the last 20 years and looking at where we are right now, I think we're more at the beginning of what the hand-held revolution is going to mean. And we probably can't understand what it's going to be like 20 years from now, but it's going to be amazing.

Dennis Moran: Principal, Dennis Moran Design

To some degree many people do today, not me but a lot of young people, are basically living their life from their phone. It certainly looks like we're moving towards a single platform, a single mobile device of some character. Who knows what that will be? Whether it's the next-generation iPad or the next iteration of a smart phone, it seems like there is an incredible convergence of media, and it does seem like it's converging into some single hardware device that will become the core of our everyday life.

Paige Beal: Assistant Professor, Marketing & Advertising, Point Park University

Hand-held mobile. Right now, you have to pry it out of my cold, dead hands, and I think particularly from a younger demographic that's going to be evolving. That's where the advance is going to be. That individual one to one, the entity that hangs with you, and it does everything—maybe it is a jack in the back of your head at some point. It doesn't look that far-fetched these days. I'm not sure if that's good or bad, but that kind of being embedded, whether it be figuratively or literally, seems to be where we're going with the Internet.

Guido D'Elia: Partner, Mind Over Media

If I knew I'd bet on it. I have no clue, but I would think that mobile devices probably would do things that we have no idea right now, and they would be in the palm of everyone's hand. Sitting here today, that looks like that would be it, but five years from now we may say "Where did that come from?"

Brian Bronaugh: President/Executive Creative Director, Mullen – Pittsburgh

I was listening to Roma Manual speak in a conference in New York, and he posed a question very similar to this one. He said the only thing that you can predict in the political process is that it'll be unpredictable, and I would apply the same tactic to the question about our business. That's the only thing I could predict, and I'm always weary of saying "It shall be so; it's going to be this way."

The unpredictability of where we're going is the norm, and the only thing I find comfort or solace in is when it gets back to, "can we tell a good story? Can we deliver an authentic and relevant message for our clients?" As long as we have that as a base foundation, predicting how we do that and what channels we're going to go through is done on a year-by-year basis.

Rob Deaner: Founder/Composer, Market Street Sound

It's kind of the Wild West again. Where it's going: smaller, better, faster, you know? No clue. Who knows? Do you know?

Discussion Questions

1. Do you agree or disagree with James Carey that technology does not actually make our lives better? Why or why not?

2. Can personalized product recommendations go too far? Will we grow more comfortable with this approach to advertising in the future? Why or why not?

3. What was the most significant advancement in communications in the last 20 years? Why?

4. Przyborski identified the computer as the most significant advancement in the last 20 years, citing the increasing affordability of technology like cameras, computers, and editing software as major developments. He said, "You can produce a network TV show or a network grade TV spot with just those two devices if you have the talent." If this trend continues, will we compete more on talent than on resources? Why or why not?

5. What will be the most significant advancement in communications in the next 20 years? Why?

6. Many of our panelists argued that the future was unpredictable. Is there value in trying to predict the future of our industry? Why or why not?

7. Moran predicted that, based on current trends, a singular mobile device "will become the core of our everyday life." Do you agree? Why or why not?

8. Predict the future: How will we most likely communicate in 20 years?

Join the Conversation

Scan the QR codes from this section to watch the video for each question, then read the comments shared by others in our community. Add your thoughts to join our conversation.

Q19 | What is most significant advancement for communications in the last 20 years?

Q20 | What will impact communications over the next 20 years?

All of us who professionally use the mass media are the shapers of society. We can vulgerize that society. We can brutalize it. Or we can help lift it onto a higher level.

- Bill Bernbach, American Advertising Creative Director

On the set of *20YEARS Communications*, a 20-video series produced by Ideahaus. Photo courtesy of Jack Wolf.

Sources

Introduction

Popović, K., (July 2005). *The Theory of Communitivity*. http://ideahaus.com/community/2004/05/05/the-theory-of-communitivity/

Chapter 01

Bidwell, M. & Mollick, E., (July 2012). *Entrepreneurial Careers and Happiness*. Whart Entrepreneurship Blog. http://beacon.wharton.upenn.edu/entrepreneurship

Binder, M. & Coad, A., (Jan. 2012). *Life Satisfaction and self-employment: a matching approach*. Small Business Economics.1-25.

Fonner, K.L. & Roloff, M.E., (2010). *Why Teleworkers are More Satisfied with Their Jobs than are Office-Based Workers: When Less Contact is Beneficial*. Journal of Applied Communications. 38(4), 336-361.

Friedman, T.L., (2007). *The World is Flat 3.0: A Brief History of the Twenty-first Century*. Picador, United Kingdom.

Gibbons, J.M., (Jan. 2010). *I Can't Get No... Job Satisfaction, That is*. The Conference Board.

Global Workplace Analytics and the Telework Research Network, (June 2011). The Latest Telecommuting Statistics. http://teleworkresearchnetwork.com

Society for Human Resource Management, (2011). *2011 Employee Job Satisfaction and Engagement: Gratification and Commitment to Work in a Sluggish Economy*. http://www.shrm.org/

Chapter 02

Berlo, D.K., (1960). *The Process of Communication: An Introduction to Theory and Practice*. Holt, Rinehart, and Winston: New York.

D'Abate, C., (May, 2010). *Developmental Interactions for Business Students: Do They Make a Difference*? Journal of Leadership & Organizational Studies, 17(2). 143-155.

Givens, T., (2 Oct. 2009). *The Importance of Mentors*. Inside Higher Ed. http://www.insidehighered.com/advice/running/givens3

Hays, T., Minichiello, V., & Wright, P., (Dec. 2000). *Mentorship: the Meaning of the Relationships for Musicians.* Research Studies in Music Education, 15(1). 3-14.

Shannon, C.E. & Weaver, W., (1949). *The Mathematical Theory of Communication*. University of Illinois Press.

Schatz, E., (Nov. 1999). *Mentors: Matchmaking for Young People*. Journal of Advanced Academics, 11(2). 67-87.

Wolff, H. & Moser, K. (Dec. 2008). *Effects of Networking on Career Success: A Longitudinal Study*. Laser Discussion Papers, 24. University of Erlangen-Nuremberg.

Chapter 03

Austin, E.W. & Pinkleton, B.E. (2009). *Strategic Public Relations Management*. New York, NY: Routledge.

Bernthal, P.R., (2001). *Recruitment and Selection. Development Dimension International & Electronic Recruiting Exchange*. http://www.ddiworld.com/DDIWorld/media/trend-research/recruitment-and-selection_ere_es_ddi.pdf?ext=.pdf

Broom, G.M. & Dozier, D.M. (1990). *Using research in public relations: Applications to program management.* Englewood Cliffs, NJ: Prentice-Hall.

Collins, J., (Oct. 2006). *Good to Great: Why Some Companies Make the Leap... and Other's Don't*. HarperBusiness: New York, NY.

Doherty-Sneddon, G. et al, (1997). *Face-to-face and video mediated communication: a comparison of dialogue structure and task performance*. Journal of Experimental Psychology-applied. 3(2). 105-125.

Flaherty, L.M., Pearce, K.J., & Rubin, R.B., (1998). *Internet and face-to-face communication: Not functional alternatives.* Communications Quarterly, 46(3). 250-268. Hart Research Associates, (2010). Raising the Bar: Employers' Views on College Learning In the Wake of The Economic Downturn. The Association of American Colleges and Universities. http://www.aacu.org/leap/documents/2009_EmployerSurvey.pdf

Ofcom, (18 July 2012). *UK is now texting more than talking*. Ofcom. http://media.ofcom.org.uk/2012/07/18/uk-is-now-texting-more-than-talking/

Olson, G.M. & Olson, J.S., (2000). *Distance Matters*. Human Computer Interaction. 15. 139-178.

Rogers, E.M. & Kincaid, D.L. (1981). *Communication networks: Toward a new paradigm for research*. New York, NY: Free Press.

Werner, T. (11 May 2011). *Photography Isn't Dead, The Business Model Is.* Strictly Business Blog, American Society of Media Photographers. http://www.asmp.org/strictlybusiness/2011/05/photography-isnt-dead-the-business-model-is/#.UFeSgo1mSIQ

Chapter 04

Godin, S. (1999). *Permission Marketing: Turning Strangers Into Friends and Friends Into Customers*. New York, NY: Simon & Schuster.

Godin, S. (2001). *Unleashing the IdeaVirus*. New York, NY: Hyperion.

Grimes, M. (10 April 2012). Neilsen: *Global Consumers' Trust in 'Earned' Advertising Grows in Importance*. Neilsen. http://www.nielsen.com/us/en/insights/press-room/2012/nielsen-global-consumers-trust-in-earned-advertising-grows.html

Kilbourne, J. (1999). *Deadly Persuasion: Why Women and Girls Must Fight the Addictive Power of Advertising*. New York, NY: Free Press.

Li, C. & Bernoff, J. (2011). *Groundswell, Expanded and Revised Edition: Winning a World Transformed by Social Technologies*. Boston, MA: Harvard Business Review Press.

Locke, C., Levine, R., Searls, D., & Weinberger, D. (2000). *The Cluetrain Manifesto: The End of Business as Usual*. New York, NY: Basic Books.

McNair, B. (2004). *PR Must Die: Spin, Anti-Spin and Political Public Relations in the UK*, 1997-2004. Journalism Studies, 5(3). 325-338.

Miller, D. & Dinan, W. (2008). *A Century of Spin: How Public Relations Became the Cutting Edge of Corporate Power*. London, UK: Pluto Press.

Morales, L. (29 Sept. 2010). *Distrust in U.S. Media Edges Up to Record High*. Gallup Politics. http://www.gallup.com/poll/143267/Distrust-Media- Edges-Record-High.aspx

Pew Research Center (13 Sept. 2009). *Press Accuracy Rating Hits Two Decade Low: Public Evaluations of the News Media: 1985-2009*. Pew Research Center for the People & the Press. http://www.people-press.org/2009/09/13/press-accuracy-rating-hits-two-decade-low/

Pew Research Center (2012). *Demographics of Internet Users. Pew Internet & American Life Project*. http://pewinternet.org/Static-Pages/Trend-Data-(Adults)/Whos-Online.aspx

Pew Research Center (6 June 2012). *Older Adults and Internet Use. Pew Internet & American Life Project*. http://pewinternet.org/Reports/2012/Older-adults-and-internet-use.aspx

Pew Research Center (17 Sept. 2012). *Pew Internet: Social Networking. Pew Internet & American Life Project*. http://pewinternet.org/Commentary/2012/March/Pew-Internet-Social-Networking-full-detail.aspx

Soh, H., Reid, L.N., & King, K.W. (Sept. 2007). *Trust in Different Advertising*

Media. Journalism & Mass Communication Quarterly. 84(3). 455-476.

Stauber, J. & Rampton, S. (1 July 2002). *Toxic Sludge is Good for You: Lies, Damn Lies and the Public Relations Industry*. Monroe, ME: Common Courage Press.

Sut, J. (Producer & Director). (1999). *Killing Us Softly 3: Advertising's Image of Women*. USA: Media Education Foundation.

Chapter 05

Grefé, R. (12 Oct. 2010). *How do Business Balance Crowd Participation and Design?* American Institute of Graphic Arts. http://www.aiga.org/how-do- businesses-balance-crowd-participation-and-design/

Hirth, M., Hobfeld, T., & Tran-Gia, P. (February 2011). *Human Cloud as Emerging Internet Application – Anatomy of the Microworkers Crowdsourcing Platform*. University of Wurzburg, Institute of Computer Science. http://www3.informatik.uni-wuerzburg.de/TR/tr478.pdf

Ipeirotis, P.G., Provost, F., & Wang, J. (2010). *Quality Management on Amazon Mechanical Turk.* Leonard N. Stern School of Business, New York University. http://people.stern.nyu.edu/panos/publications/hcomp2010.pdf

Kurzweil, R. (January 2000). *The Age of Spiritual Machines: When Computers Exceed Human Intelligence*. New York, NY: Penguin.

Perez-Pena, R. (27 Oct. 2008). *Newspaper Circulation Continues to Decline Rapidly*. The New York Times. http://www.nytimes.com/2008/10/28/ business/media/28circ.html

Pew Research Center's Project for Excellence in Journalism, (2011). *Magazines: By the Numbers. The State of the News Media 2011: An Annual Report on American Journalism*. http://stateofthemedia.org/2011/magazines- essay/data-page-4/

Pew Research Center's Project for Excellence in Journalism, (2011). *Newspapers: By the Numbers. The State of the News Media 2011: An*

Annual Report on American Journalism. http://stateofthemedia.org/2011/newspapers-essay/data-page-6/

Pew Research Center's Project for Excellence in Journalism, (2011). *Local TV: By the Numbers. The State of the News Media 2011: An Annual Report on American Journalism*. http://stateofthemedia.org/2011/local-tv-essay/data-page-3/

Pew Research Center's Project for Excellence in Journalism, (2011). *Cable TV: By the Numbers. The State of the News Media 2011: An Annual Report on American Journalism*. http://stateofthemedia.org/2011/cable-essay/data-page-2/

Pew Research Center's Project for Excellence in Journalism, (2011). *Network: By the Numbers. The State of the News Media 2011: An Annual Report on American Journalism*. http://stateofthemedia.org/2011/network-essay/data-page-5/

Ranade, G. & Varshney, L.R. (2012). *To Crowdsource Or Not to Crowdsource?* Human Computation: AAAI Technical Report. http://www.aaai.org/ocs/index.php/WS/AAAIW12/paper/viewFile/5241/5619

Ross, J., Zaldivar, A., Irani, L., Tomlinson, B., & Silberman, M.S. (10 April 2010). *Who are the Crowdworkers? Shifting Demographics in Mechanical Turk*. CHI 2010. http://www.ics.uci.edu/~jwross/pubs/RossEtAl-WhoAreTheCrowdworkers -altCHI2010.pdf

Solon, O. (2 July 2012). *Freelancer.com's CEO Matt Barrie's mission to create the 'eBay of jobs.'* Wired.co.uk. http://www.wired.co.uk/news/archive/2012-07/02/freelancercom-matt-barrie

The Center for the Digital Future: USC Annenberg School, (Jan. 2012). *Special Report: America at the Digital Turning Point*. Digitialcenter.org. http://annenberg.usc.edu/News%20and%20Events/News/~/media/PDFs/CDF_ DigitalReport.ashx

Chapter 06

Carey, J.W. (Sept. 2008). *Communication as Culture, Revised Edition: Essays on Media and Society*. New York, NY: Routledge.

Duhigg, C. (16 Feb. 2012). *How Companies Learn Your Secrets*. The New York Times. http://www.nytimes.com/2012/02/19/magazine/shopping-habits.html?smid=pl-share

Goff, N. (September 2011). *Direct-Response Bookselling: How it Died, Why it is Alive Again, and Why It Will Become Even More Important in the Future.* Publishing Research Quarterly, 27(3), 259-267.

Jenkins, H. (March 2004). *The Cultural Logic of Media Convergence*. International Journal of Cultural Studies, 7(1).

"They ask me, 'how is the best way to communicate?' I said, 'Tell the people who you are and what you do.' Hi, I'm Jack Wolf, and I'm a photographer. You can call me at 412-963-7915." - Jack Wolf

Index

D

E

F

G

H

I

J

K

L

M

N

O

P

R

V

W

Y

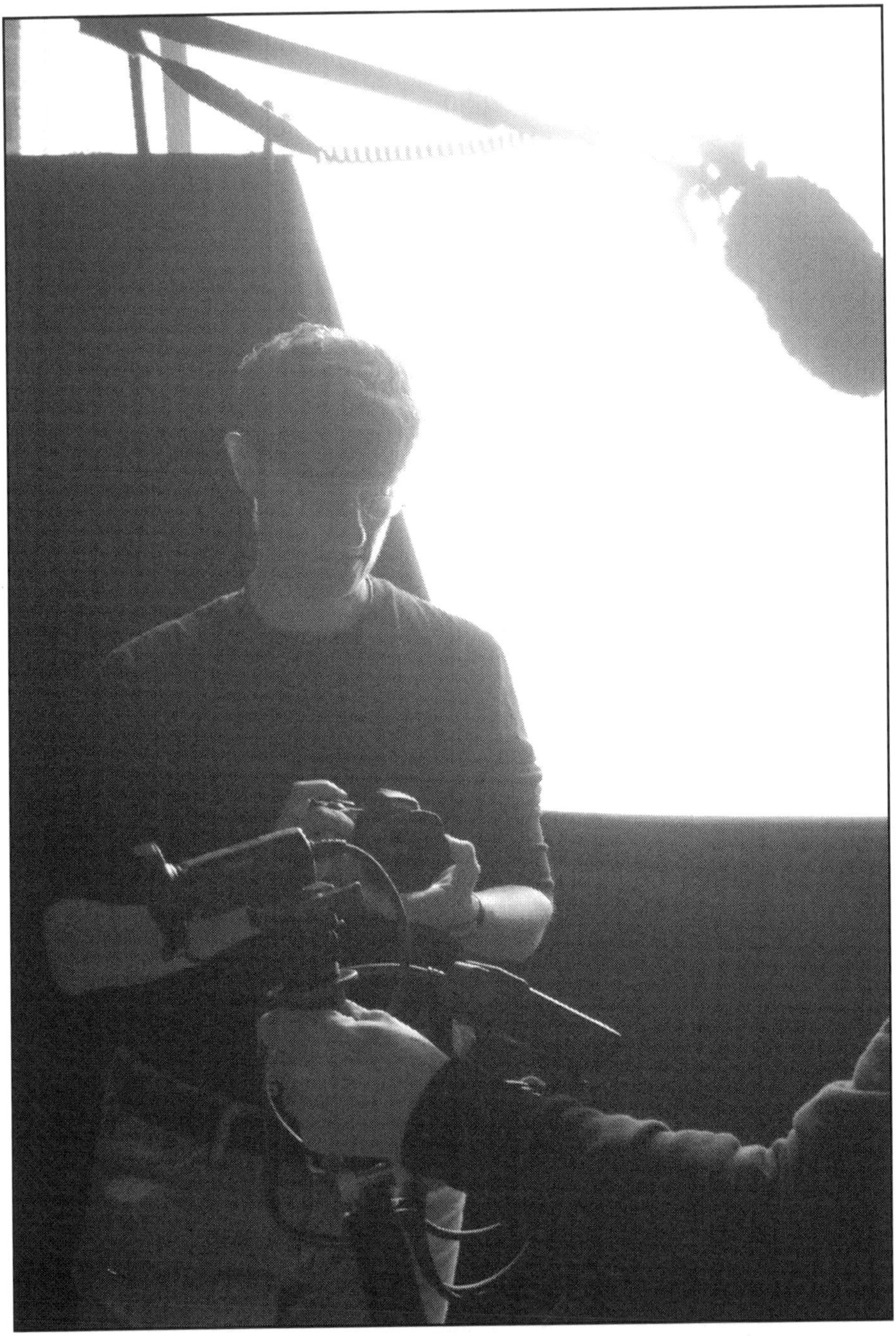

Special thanks to Amy King for producing *20YEARS Communications*.
Photo courtesy of Jack Wolf.

Glossary

Account Management
A service provided by agencies to clients which includes the management of the business between the two companies as well as the communications planning and creative development requirements of the client.

Account Planning
A process which considers the quantitative and qualitative information of target audiences during the development of a communications plan for a business. Also referred to as brand planning or strategic planning.

Account Service
The department within an agency that is responsible for the day-to-day management of client interests and resources. Roles include Account Executives and Project Managers.

Adobe Illustrator
Part of the Adobe Systems Creative Suite, Adobe Illustrator is a multi-platform software application, ideal for creating 2-D and 3-D web vector graphics and artwork. Illustrator is used to create and edit graphics and optimize images in a professional environment.

Adobe Photoshop
Part of the Adobe Systems Creative Suite, Adobe Photoshop is a multi-platform software application that has become the definitive solution for professional web photo editing and artwork creation. Photoshop is used to create and edit photos and graphics and to optimize images.

Advertising
A form of communication used to educate, inform or persuade an audience to respond to a call to action. Advertising channels include television, radio, outdoor, print and online. Most frequently, advertising is used to move consumers to purchase a product or service or to respond to a call to action.

Advocates
Consumers whose brand loyalty moves them to suggest a product or service to others.

Analog Modem
One of the first devices used to connect to the Internet, an analog modem converts digital pulses to tones in order to transmit information via telephone lines.

Apps
An abbreviation for a specific application that provides a useful task to the user. Apps are commonly found on smartphones and tablet computers and other mobile devices. Available through distribution platforms, apps are downloaded to the target device.

Audience
A specific group of people within a target market identified to sell a product or service. An audience is described by combining age, gender, marital status, education, geographic location, etc. Identifying an appropriate target audience is considered the most critical activity in communications.

B2B
An acronym for "business to business," B2B describes the business transactions between businesses, like a wholesaler and a retailer.

B2C
An acronym for "business to consumers," B2C describes the common retail business transaction between a business and the end-user.

Bandwidth
The rate of data transmitted over a network measured in bits per second (bps), sometimes used to refer to a team or individual's available capacity to complete a task or project.

Branding
A marketing practice which involves the creation of a name, term, symbol or design that identifies a product or service and separates it from similar products or services. Often considered the most valuable asset of an organization, companies manage their brands to maximize their value in the marketplace.

Clients
Individuals or organizations that contract an agency or expert for communications services.

Communications
The meaningful transmission of messages using speech, visuals, signals, writing or behavior between two or more people. Communication requires a sender, message and a receiver and may be synchronous (like a conversation) or asynchronous (like an advertisement).

Communitivity
The use of interpersonal skills, technology and connectivity to facilitate the development of a personal community. Defined by Kevin Popović, personal communitivity can be thought of as the measure of the concurrent and overlapping circles of activity, both online and on-site, to create a presence.

Consumer
An individual or group that purchases a product or service produced or provided by a company for personal use.

Corporate Identity
The overall image of a business, product or service in the minds of its audiences, including customers, clients, investors or employees. Commonly, a corporate identity is recognized to include the name and logo, as well as an emotional connection, i.e., a consumer "likes" a product.

Corporate Propaganda
Intentionally manipulative communications spread by businesses. Often used to manipulate the stock market or in political advocacy. Media manipulation is the most common form of corporate propaganda.

Creative Director
A leadership role in graphic design and advertising agencies, the creative director works with copywriters, art directors, graphic designers, photographers, programmers, etc., to develop client communications.

Crowdsourcing
The practice of obtaining services, generating ideas or developing content by soliciting participation from a group of people, usually from an online community.

Design
The conception of a plan or convention which influences and guides the construction of an object or a system, sometimes used as a synonym for graphic design.

Desktop Publishing
Often abbreviated as DTP, desktop publishing is the creation of documents using a computer and a page layout program. The term was created in 1983 with the introduction of the Apple LaserWriter printer and exploded with introduction of Aldus' PageMaker software which produced typographic quality comparable to traditional cost-prohibitive printing.

Digital Strategist
A person within the marketing department who leads the development of digital initiatives for an organization. Their focus includes customer intelligence, web site development, social media, mobile, e-Commerce, search engine optimization and advertising.

DVR
An acronym for digital video recorder, commonly used to automate the process of recording television content.

E-Commerce
Also known as electronic commerce, e-commerce is an industry that facilitates the buying and selling of products and services using electronic systems, like the Internet. E-commerce includes the use of mobile commerce, electronic funds transfer, online transaction processing, inventory management and customer management.

Facebook

An online social media networking service founded by Mark Zuckerberg in 2004. With more than 1 billion users (March 2013) Facebook is the largest social media network.

Flash

Formerly known as Macromedia Flash, flash is a platform for creating graphics, games and animations for multimedia-rich web applications.

Flash Mobs

A coordinated effort to assemble a large group of people in a public place, usually for the purposes of humor.

Flickr

An image and video hosting website and community acquired by Yahoo! in 2005. The service is most commonly used by bloggers to embed photographs and share them across social media.

Fortune 500 Company

A list compiled by Fortune Magazine ranking the top 500 public corporations by gross revenue.

G-Chat

An online text communication application provided by Google.

Google

An American-based company providing Internet-related products and services, including search, software and online advertising technologies. Its mission statement includes, "to organize the world's information and make it universally accessible and useful."

Google Wave

A short-lived Google product for real-time collaborative editing.

Groundswell

An accumulation of a shared opinion among a large group of people; a term popularized by a book of the same name written by Charlene Li and Josh Bernoff.

Hulu
An online streaming video service that includes television shows, movies and independently created content.

Ideavirus
An idea or behavior that spreads within a culture, a term popularized by a book of the same name written by Seth Godin.

Ideation
The process of forming, collecting or generating new ideas.

Illustration
A depiction, such as a painting, drawing, photograph or other image.

Internet
A global system of linked computer networks that use the standard Internet Protocol Suite (TCP/IP) and that helps billions of users to share content and to communicate. The Internet supports information services, like hypertext documents of the World Wide Web (WWW) and the infrastructure for email.

Interrotron
A production tool used in documentaries. Two teleprompters are connected to two cameras. Camera A is rolling on the subject, and Camera B is simply feeding Camera A's prompter, allowing for the subject to be looking directly into the interviewer's eyes through the beam splitter as they are being interviewed.

iPad
A line of tablet computers developed by Apple which run the Apple iOS. First released in 2010, the user interface popularized a multi-touch screen and a virtual keyboard for personal computing.

iPhone
A line of mobile phones developed by Apple which run the Apple iOS and that defined the smartphone industry. The iPhone is attributed to helping make Apple one of the most valuable publicly traded companies in 2011.

iPod
A line of portable media devices produced by Apple used to access music, photos, videos, games and information.

Journalism
The profession of preparing written, visual or audio material in preparation for dissemination through public media, originally intended to inform society about issues, current events and topics of interest.

Kickstarter
A crowdfunding web site that provides tools for entrepreneurs and independent projects, like films, music, video games and non-profit ventures.

Mad Men
A popular AMC television drama series that focuses on the lives of Madison Avenue advertising agencies in the 1960s.

Marketing
The process of communicating the value of a product or service to customers within a marketplace for the purpose of creating a sale. This includes the use of science to select target markets by using market analysis and segmentation as well as understanding consumer behavior.

Marketing Director
The corporate executive that leads and coordinates marketing efforts for a company or organization. This role is often seen as a prime importance within the organization, providing information that helps guide other departments toward a common goal.

Mass Media
The collective term for communication mediums designed to reach large audiences, including broadcast, film, video games, radio, Internet, print and outdoor media.

Media
A generic term for communication medium, sometimes used synonymously with mass media. Also used to describe the storage and transmission of information or data.

Media Buying

A process in advertising whereby media real estate is obtained for both optimal placement and optimal price. The main responsibility of a media buyer is to identify the best price and placement to reach the target audience.

Media Convergence

The evolution of media and mediums to evolve toward a singular common platform.

Media Fragmentation

A trend toward an increasingly diverse number of channels and mediums for consuming media resulting in the decreasing number of people in each audience. For media buyers, this means they must purchase more advertising channels to reach the needed number of customers than before.

Media Planning

The process that an agency uses to determine the best combination of media to achieve a client's goals or objectives.

Metrics

The collection of data related to the reach and effectiveness of communications efforts for the purpose of measurement and analysis.

Mobile

A category characterized by portable, battery-powered products, including cell phones, smart phones, and tablets.

MP3

A popular encoding format that produces compressed digital audio files. MP3 is the standard of digital audio compression for the playback of music on most digital audio players, smart phones and tablets.

Multimedia

Media and content that uses a combination of different content forms, including a combination of text, audio, still images, animation, video or interactivity content forms.

MySpace
A social networking service known for its emphasis on music. From 2005 to 2008, MySpace was the most visited social networking site in the world. It is credited with significantly influencing music, gaming and the use of unique URLs for artists.

Networking
The process of developing a social network with others who share similar personal interests or business objectives using a profile, personal information, content and online activity.

Newgrounds
An entertainment website dedicated primarily to hosting and sharing Adobe Flash animations and games.

New Media
An abstract term that refers to digital media that rose to popularity after traditional media like television, radio and print had been established.

Outsource
Contracting an internal business process outside of a company.

Permission Marketing
Refers to the process of getting a customer's permission to contact them with future marketing messages, usually via email; coined by Seth Godin.

Pinterest
A social photo-sharing website that allows users to create theme-based image collections. Users browse other boards for images and "re-pin" (share) images to create their own boards of interest.

Podcasting
A series of digital media episodes including audio, video and information. Users subscribe to content using web-syndication services and a computer or mobile device.

Post-production
The last stage of the production process for film, video and photography during the production of motion pictures, films, television, radio, advertising commercials, audio recordings, photography and other digital products.

Pre-production
The process of planning and preparing all of the elements used in the production of motion pictures, films, television, radio, advertising commercials, audio recordings, photography and other digital products.

Process
A premeditated series of steps taken to achieve a result.

Production
The act of performing and recording motion pictures, films, television, radio, advertising commercials, audio recordings, photography and other digital products.

Public Relations
Also known as "PR," public relations is the development and management of information and opinion of an individual, business or organization and the public via media and events.

Recording Engineer
A recording engineer records, mixes and reproduces sound for commercial purposes.

Research
The methodical search for insight into a topic or issue for the purpose of obtaining new information and making informed decisions.

Return on Investment
The perceived gain for the resources spent on an effort, return on investment typically refers to financial capital but can also refer to more abstract rewards like increased awareness and loyalty or the growth of a social good; also called R.O.I.

Rhetoric
The art of persuasion through speaking or writing.

Sales
The process of identifying a prospect, introducing a product or service, and creating an exchange for money.

Satellite Marketing
Developed by Kevin Popović, satellite marketing is a communications strategy designed to connect an organization with its target markets via social media sites and services. These social media sites and services act as marketing sub-stations, or "satellites." Satellites are used in addition to, or in place of, traditional media, such as print, radio, television, direct and outdoor advertising. The goal of satellite marketing is to expand the reach of the organization and to enhance the results by creating relationships.

Saturation
The diffusion of a product or service in the market, is sometimes used to suggest over-saturation. The level of saturation can depend on variables like price, competition and consumer purchasing power.

SMS
Short message service (SMS) is the text messaging component of mobile communications that enables the exchange of messages between land lines and mobile devices.

Social Media
A set of virtual communities and networks that provides the means of interaction and exchange among members. Through the mutual sharing of information and user-generated content, social media interactions have become a mainstay of modern communications.

Spin
Sometimes compared with propaganda, spin describes the act of creatively presenting information to intentionally manipulate or deceive the public.

Target Audience
A specific group of people within a target market.

Technological Convergence
The evolution of technological systems moving toward similar platforms and tasks.

Telecommuting
Also known as remote work or telework, telecommuting is an off-site working relationship where workers are physically located at home, on location or on-site as needed. Workers use mobile computing and telecommunications to interact with other workers.

Traditional Media
The collection of media that existed prior to the Internet, traditional media includes television, radio, film, music, newspapers, magazines and books.

Tumblr
A short-form microblogging platform which allows users to post multimedia content. Purchased by Yahoo! in 2013 for $1.1 billion.

Twitter
A social networking site and microblogging service where users can send and receive posts - known as "tweets" - which are limited to 140 characters.

Typography
The art of setting or arranging type for printing, including the selection of typefaces, point size, leading, tracking and kerning.

Unique Selling Proposition
Also known as USP, , unique selling proposition is a marketing concept developed by Rossar Reeves that proposed advertisers present unique propositions to the consumer to help convince them to convert brand choices.

Vendor
A person or company who offers a product or service to a company.

Wi-Fi
A wireless Internet network or the use of radio waves to transmit data wirelessly between electronic and mobile devices on a network.

WordPress
An open source content management system (CMS) used for blogs and for websites, ranked as the most popular blogging system in the world (2013).

YouTube
A video sharing website where users can upload, view and share video using HTML5 technology to display user-generated movies, short films, educational programs, television shows and music videos.

Kevin Popović, Founder & CEO of Ideahaus.
Photo courtesy of Cece Canton.

Connect with the Author

Kevin Popović is the Founder & CEO of Ideahaus, a boutique creative communications agency with studios in Pittsburgh and San Diego. Since 1990, he has helped clients figure out what to say and how to say it to their target markets.

Scan these QR codes to connect with Kevin Popović, follow @KevinPopovic on social media or visit http://ideahaus.com.

Connect on LinkedIn

Follow on Twitter @KevinPopovic

Add on Google+ Kevin Popovic

In the modern world of business, it is useless to be a creative, original thinker unless you can also sell what you create.

- David Ogilvy, Father of Modern Advertising

http://ideahaus.com/20YEARS

25547010R00119

Made in the USA
Lexington, KY
27 August 2013